SCOTT FORESMAN ENGLISH

IN CONTACT

2

BEGINNING

Second Edition

Jane Sturtevant

Longman

In Contact 2, Second Edition

Pearson Education, 10 Bank Street, White Plains, NY 10606

Editorial directors: Louise Jennewine, Allen Ascher
Acquisitions editor: Bill Preston
Director of design and production: Rhea Banker
Development editor: Laura Le Dréan
Production manager: Alana Zdinak
Production supervisor: Liza Pleva
Managing editor: Linda Moser
Senior production editor: Virginia Bernard
Production editor: Christine Lauricella
Senior manufacturing manager: Patrice Fraccio
Manufacturing supervisor: Edith Pullman
Photo research: Quarasan and Aerin Csigay
Cover design: Charles Yuen
Text design and composition: Quarasan
Photo and illustration credits: See p. vi.

Library of Congress Cataloging-in-Publication Data

Sturtevant, Jane
   In contact. 2 / Jane Sturtevant.—2nd ed.
      p.   cm.—(ScottForesman English)
   ISBN 0-201-57981-2
   1. English language textbooks for foreign speakers.   I. Title.
II. Series.
PE1128.S894   1999   99-33873
428.2′4—dc21   CIP

2 3 4 5 6 7 8 9 10–PO–04 03 02 01 00

CONTENTS

Starting Out vii
- *To use greetings and introductions*
- *To exchange personal information*
- *To review the present tense of* to be

UNIT 1 Lifestyles 1
- *To talk about lifestyles*
- *To talk about routines and schedules*
- *To talk about frequency*

UNIT 2 Personalities 11
- *To describe personalities*
- *To discuss likes and dislikes*
- *To express preferences*
- *To make suggestions*

UNIT 3 Where We Live 21
- *To describe homes*
- *To talk about the future*
- *To discuss location*

REVIEW (Units 1–3) 31

UNIT 4 On the Job 33
- *To describe occupations*
- *To express obligation*
- *To express sequence*

UNIT 5 Would You Do Me a Favor? . . 43
- *To make polite requests*
- *To offer help*
- *To ask for help*

UNIT 6 Turning Points 53
- *To talk about one's life*
- *To talk about the past*
- *To talk about past abilities*
- *To sequence information*

REVIEW (Units 4–6) 63

UNIT 7 Are You Hungry? 65
- *To talk about food and eating*
- *To use count and non-count nouns*
- *To use quantifiers*
- *To use linking verbs*

UNIT 8 Accidents Will Happen 75
- *To talk about what was happening*
- *To express time relationships*
- *To give reasons and describe results*

UNIT 9 Love That Style! 85
- *To describe clothing*
- *To compare and contrast*
- *To express preferences*
- *To ask for and give opinions*

REVIEW (Units 7–9) 95

UNIT 10 Getting Away 97
- *To read maps and give directions*
- *To describe location*
- *To express conditions*
- *To talk about plans*
- *To convince someone of an idea*

UNIT 11 Art for Art's Sake 107
- *To describe how people do things*
- *To express possession*
- *To state opinions*
- *To disagree*

UNIT 12 What's the Matter? 117
- *To ask for and give advice*
- *To complain*
- *To use reflexive pronouns*

REVIEW (Units 10–12) 127

Irregular Verbs 129
International Phonetic Alphabet . . 131
Unit Vocabulary 132
Index 136

SUMMARY OF SKILLS

Theme	Grammar	Listening and Speaking	Reading and Writing
Unit 1 **Lifestyles** Page 1	Simple Present with Adverbs of Frequency	**Listening:** A Radio Interview ➡ Predicting Information **Pronunciation:** –s/–es endings **Speaking:** Lifestyles ➡ Asking Someone to Speak Louder	**Reading:** Vera—On the Road Again ➡ Getting the Main Idea **Writing:** A Letter ➡ Discovering Ideas
Unit 2 **Personalities** Page 11	Gerunds *It* + Infinitive	**Listening:** Who's Coming to Dinner? ➡ Completing a Chart **Pronunciation:** Syllables **Speaking:** Saturday Plans ➡ Making Suggestions	**Reading:** Pen Pals Wanted ➡ Skimming **Writing:** Letter to a Pen Pal ➡ Evaluating a Letter
Unit 3 **Where We Live** Page 21	The Future with *Will*; The Future with *Be going to*; *Too* and *Not … enough* with Adjectives	**Listening:** Welcome to the White House! ➡ Using Pictures to Predict Content **Pronunciation:** Stressed Syllables **Speaking:** An Interesting House ➡ Taking Turns	**Reading:** Steven's Letter ➡ Scanning **Writing:** A Letter ➡ Answering *Wh–* questions to Gather Information

Review Units 1–3

Theme	Grammar	Listening and Speaking	Reading and Writing
Unit 4 **On the Job** Page 33	*Before, After, When*; *Have to/Has to*	**Listening:** Career Counseling ➡ Using the Title, Picture, and Charts to Predict Content **Pronunciation:** Stressed Words **Speaking:** Guess the Job ➡ Responding to Guesses	**Reading:** Sylvia Earle's Deep-Water Career ➡ Sequencing **Writing:** Observations ➡ Looking for Details
Unit 5 **Would You Do Me a Favor?** Page 43	Direct and Indirect Objects	**Listening:** Party Plans ➡ Taking Notes **Pronunciation:** Intonation with *Wh–* Questions **Speaking:** Plan a Party! ➡ Refusing a Request	**Reading:** Urban Homesteading ➡ Guessing the Meaning of New Words **Writing:** Asking a Favor ➡ Using a Model
Unit 6 **Turning Points** Page 53	Asking Questions About the Past; Asking About Past Ability	**Listening:** A Family Conversation ➡ Knowing the Speakers and the Situation **Pronunciation:** –ed endings **Speaking:** My Past ➡ Checking Information	**Reading:** The Great Wallendas: At Home in the Air ➡ Scanning for Important Information **Writing:** A Bio ➡ Ordering Past Events

Review Units 4–6

Theme	Grammar	Listening and Speaking	Reading and Writing
Unit 7 **Are You Hungry?** Page 65	Count/Non-count Nouns; Specific and Non-specific Quantities	**Listening:** Making Chicken Cacciatore ➡ Predicting Content **Pronunciation:** Intonation: words in a List **Speaking:** Who Will Buy What? ➡ Asking Someone to Speak Slowly	**Reading:** The Food Pyramid ➡ Using Pictures **Writing:** A Journal ➡ Listing and Ordering Items
Unit 8 **Accidents Will Happen** Page 75	Past Progressive Tense; *When* and *While* Clauses; *Because* and *So* Clauses	**Listening:** A Traffic Accident ➡ Listening for Sequence **Pronunciation:** Linking Final Consonants to Vowels **Speaking:** Whose Fault Was It? ➡ Disagreeing Politely	**Reading:** Bed and Breakfast ... and a Fire ➡ Understanding the Main Ideas **Writing:** An Accident Report ➡ Answering Information Questions
Unit 9 **Love That Style!** Page 85	Sequence of Adjectives; *As* + adjective + *as*; *Better than/Worse than*	**Listening:** What Do *You* Want? ➡ Predicting Feelings **Pronunciation:** Intonation: *or* **Speaking:** Traveling and Buying Presents ➡ Asking for Opinions	**Reading:** Catalog Shopping ➡ Scanning **Writing:** Ordering From a Catalog ➡ Including Necessary Information

Review Units 7–9

Theme	Grammar	Listening and Speaking	Reading and Writing
Unit 10 **Getting Away** Page 97	Present Progressive: Future Meaning; Clauses with *If*	**Listening:** When Can We Get Together? ➡ Listening to Complete a Chart **Pronunciation:** Thought Groups **Speaking:** Planning a Vacation ➡ Convincing Someone of a Plan	**Reading:** Vacation Brochures ➡ Scanning **Writing:** An Invitation ➡ Including Necessary Information
Unit 11 **Art for Art's Sake** Page 107	*Whose* and Possessive Pronouns; Adverbs	**Listening:** Are You Serious? ➡ Previewing the Topic **Pronunciation:** Reductions **Speaking:** Talking about Art ➡ Disagreeing Strongly	**Reading:** Changing Ideas about Art ➡ Understanding Reference Words **Writing:** An e-mail Letter ➡ Understanding e-mail
Unit 12 **What's the Matter?** Page 117	Reflexive Pronouns	**Listening:** Hello, You're on *Health Line* ➡ Predicting the Topic **Pronunciation:** Unstressed *he, him, her,* and *his* **Speaking:** Problems and Advice ➡ Giving Advice	**Reading:** Ask Kit and Kat ➡ Getting the General Idea **Writing:** A Letter Asking for Advice ➡ Explaining a Problem

Review Units 10–12

ACKNOWLEDGMENTS

Our thanks to the following piloters and reviewers whose comments and suggestions were of great value in the development of the second edition of *Scott Foresman English:*

Angie Alcocer, Maria Alvarado School, Lima, Peru; **Walter A. Alvarez Barreto,** Santa Teresita School, Lima, Peru; **Chuck Anderson,** Tokyo, Japan; **Elba de Buenafama,** School Hipocampitos, Los Teques-Caracas, Venezuela; **Alexandra Espinoza Cascante,** Instituto Universal de Idiomas, San Jose, Costa Rica; **Orquidea Flores** and **Romelia Perez,** Colegio Nuestra Senora de la Paz, Puerto La Cruz, Venezuela; **Brigite Fonseca,** Colegio Bom Jesus in Joinville, Santa Catarina, Brazil; **Ana Maria Garcia,** Instituto Tecnologico de Estudios Superiores de Monterrey, Mexico; **Irma K. Ghosn,** Lebanese American University, Byblos, Lebanon; **Carmina Gonzalez Molina,** Instituto Cultural, A.C., Mexico City, Mexico; **Gloria I. Gutierrez Vera,** Colegio Regiomontano Contry, Monterrey, Mexico; **Tatiana Hernandez Gaubil,** Colegio Madre del Divino Pastor, San Jose, Costa Rica; **Madeleine Hudders,** University at Puerto Rico, San Juan, Puerto Rico; **Denise Khoury,** Notre Dame de Louaize School, Lebanon; **Jane Lyon Lee,** Chungang University, Seoul, Korea; **Francisco J. Martinez,** Instituto La Salle Preparatoria, Leon, Mexico; **Paula Sanchez Cortes,** Mexico; **Nitzie de Sanley** and **Mireya Miramare,** IFISA, Puerto La Cruz, Venezuela; **Diana Yupanqui Alvarez,** San Antonio de Mujeres School, Lima, Peru

Photos: p. x, PhotoDisc, Inc.; p. 1, (l, inset, br) Corbis/AFP, (tr) Corbis/Wally McNamee; p. 27, (l) PhotoDisc, Inc., (r) Corbis/Kevin Fleming; p. 33, Corbis/Digital Stock; p. 49, PhotoDisc, Inc.; p. 50, Corbis/Joseph Sohm, ChromoSohm Inc.; p. 51, Corbis/Ted Spiegel; p. 53, The Corel Corporation; p. 57, Photo provided by MetaTools; p. 60, Corbis/Bettmann-UPI; p. 61, Michael Philip Manheim/Marilyn Gartman Agency; p. 70, Corbis/Digital Stock; p. 73, (top to bottom) (a, b) Photo provided by MetaTools, (c, d, f) PhotoDisc, Inc., (e) The Corel Corporation; p. 75, (Bkgrnd) The Corel Corporation; p. 82, PhotoDisc, Inc.; p. 83, Corbis/Wolfgang Kaehler; p. 88, Photo provided by MetaTools; p. 97, PhotoDisc, Inc.; p. 104, (l) PhotoDisc, Inc., (r) The Corel Corporation; p. 106, PhotoDisc, Inc.; p. 107, (from left to right) Wassily Kandinsky, French, b. Russian, 1866-1944, Painting with Green Center, oil on canvas, 1913, Arthur Jerome Eddy Memorial Collection, 1931.510. Photograph courtesy of The Art Institute of Chicago., Alberto Giacometti, Swiss, 1901-1966, Three Walking Men, bronze, 1948/49, Edward E. Ayer Endowment in memory of Charles L. Hutchinson, 1951.256. Photograph courtesy of the Art Institute of Chicago. © 1999 Artists Rights Society (ARS), New York/ADAGP, Paris., Frans Hals, the Laughing Cavalier. Reproduced by permission of the Trustees, the Wallace Collection, London.; p. 110, PhotoDisc, Inc.; p. 112, (left to right) Arcimboldo, Giuseppe (1527-93). Summer (Allegory), 1563. Kunsthistorisches Museum, Vienna, Austria. Erich Lessing/Art Resource, NY., Picasso, Pablo (1881-1973). Weeping Woman. 1937. Tate Gallery, London/Art Resource, NY. © 1999 Estate of Pablo Picasso/Artists Rights Society (ARS), New York.; p. 114, (top to bottom) Claude Monet, French, 1840-1926, Water Lilies, oil on canvas, 1906, Mr. And Mrs. Martin A. Ryerson Collection, 1933.1157. Photograph courtesy of The Art Institute of Chicago., Gogh, Vincent van (1853-1890). The Artist's Bedroom at Arles. Musee d'Orsay, Paris, France. Erich Lessing/Art Resource, NY.; p. 115, PhotoDisc, Inc.; p. 117, (c) Alan Schein/The Stock Market; p. 121, PhotoDisc, Inc.; p. 124, PhotoDisc, Inc.; p. 125, PhotoDisc, Inc.

Illustrations: Andrea Baruffi pp. 58, 92 (shirt), 93 (boots), 94 (jeans); Susan Blubaugh p. 66; Dan Brennan pp. 12, 17, 123; Renee Daily pp. 2, 8, 22; Felipe Galindo pp. 3, 6; T.R. Garcia pp. 35, 48; Patrick Girouard pp. viii, 5, 36, 44 (t), 90; Brian Karas pp. 18, 19, 44 (b), 45, 46; Kees de Kiefte p. 13; Jared Lee p. 11; Bob Marstall p. 34; Stephanie O'Shaughnessy p. 119; Jan Palmer p. 101; Precision Graphics pp. 99, 100; Rolin Graphics pp. 21, 98; Larry Ross pp. 39, 81; Philip Scheuer pp. vii, 85 (4 illustrations within the poloaroids), 86; Steve Schindler pp. 37, 75, 76, 108, 118; Randy Verougstraete pp. 26, 43, 97.

Cover photos: Earl Ripling/The Stock Rep (cellphone); Jim Barber/The Stock Rep (keyboard); © 1999 Jim Westphalen (type).

Introductions and Greetings

🎧 **1** These people are saying *hello* to each other. Listen to the five conversations. Write the number of the conversation in the box next to the correct people.

🎧 **2** Read the sentences. Listen again. Write the number of the conversation next to each sentence.

____	Hi, Sara.	__1__	Nice to meet you, Mei.
____	I'm from Brazil.	____	Hey, Bill! How are you?
____	Hi, Luis. I'm Siree.	____	Sara, do you know Ali?
____	Fine, thanks, Henry.	__1__	It's nice to meet you, Ms. Lee.
____	Hi! My name's Luis.	__1__	Mei, this is Ms. Lee. She's our teacher.
____	And I'm from Japan.	____	No, I don't. Hi, Ali. Nice to meet you.
____	Where are you from?		

🎧 **3** Now write the correct sentences in the bubble above each person. Listen again to check your answers.

4 These people are saying *hello*, too. Listen to their conversations. Fill in the missing words.

1. Hello, ___my___ name _____ Susanna. What's _____ name?

   David.

2. Mark, this _____ Mrs. Sato.

   How _____ you _____?

   _____ do you do?

3. Hello, Jack. _____ are you?

   _____, thanks, and you?

   Fine, _____.

4. Todd, _____ you _____ Denny?

   No. I _____. Hi, _____.

   _____, Todd.

5. Where _____ you _____?

   _____ from Jamaica.

6. Carol, do _____ _____ Patricia?

   _____, I _____. We _____ to the same school.

Review of *To be*

5 Write the correct form of *be* in the charts.

a.

I	am	from Kyoto.
He		
She		from Chicago.
It		

b.

We		
You		from Miami.
They		

c.

	I		late?
Yes,	you		.

d.

	he		a teacher?
No,	he		not.

6 Write the correct contractions.

a. he is _____*he's*_____   **f.** it is _____
b. you are _____   **g.** they are _____
c. I am _____   **h.** what is ____ _____
d. she is _____   **i.** who is _____
e. we are _____   **j.** you are not _____

Getting to Know Each Other

7 Complete the sentences. Write about *you*.

Example:

My favorite singer is *Gloria Estefan* _____.

a. My name is _____.
b. I'm from _____.
c. I was born in 19 _____.
d. My address is _____.
e. My favorite actor is _____.
f. My favorite sports are _____.

8 The sentences in Exercise 7 are answers. Write a question for each one. Use *who, what, where,* or *when*.

Example:

Who's your favorite singer?

a. _____?
b. _____?
c. _____?
d. _____?
e. _____?
f. _____?

9 Work with a partner. Ask your partner the questions from Exercise 8.
Write your partner's answers on a piece of paper.

Example:

A: What's your name?
B: My name's Raquel Rios.

10 Ask your classmates about the following activities. Who can do each
activity? Write their names on the lines.

Example:

You: Can you drive a car?
Taro: Yes, I can.

a. drive a car ____Taro____

b. ride a bike _____

c. play the piano _____

d. use a computer _____

e. speak English _____

f. make a cake _____

g. swim _____

11 Now ask about the following foods. Who likes each kind of food?
Write their names on the lines.

Example:

You: Do you like pizza?
Li-Jing: Yes, I do.

a. pizza ____Li-Jing____   e. pie _____

b. hamburgers _____   f. ice cream _____

c. hot dogs _____   g. coffee _____

d. cake _____   h. orange juice _____

Sammy Sosa

Michelle Kwan

**Venus and
Serena Williams**

Tiger Woods

GETTING STARTED

Warm Up

1 Work with a partner. Ask and answer questions about the
athletes in the photographs. Use these words.

Example:

A: What do Venus and Serena Williams do every day?

B: They play tennis.

> play baseball
> play golf
> play tennis
> skate

2 Do you know any other athletes? What sports do they play?

3 What sports do *you* play? Tell the class.

What do you do on a typical day?

4 Listen and read.

RICK: Welcome back to *Lifestyles of Real People*. I'm Rick Robinson and
I'm talking to Rina Campos, a champion skateboarder here in
Chicago. Rina, what do you do on a typical day? Do you practice
a lot with your skateboard?

Rina Campos in action

RINA: Not really. On school days, I seldom have much time. I always get up late, at about seven o'clock. I take a shower and brush my teeth, but I never eat breakfast. Well, I sometimes have a glass of milk. I usually get to school at about eight o'clock and say "hi" to my friends. Then I have classes from 8:15 a.m. to 3:15 p.m., except for lunch.

RICK: What do you usually do after school?

RINA: Well, first I go to work. I work in a music store after school. I sometimes leave early, but I usually work until the store closes at six. Then I always go home for dinner. My mother gets upset if I don't. After dinner I take my skateboard to the park and practice with my friends until eight or nine o'clock. Then I do my homework and go to bed.

RICK: So you practice about two hours a day. Do you ever practice more than that?

RINA: Oh, yes. On weekends and vacations I have a different routine. Then I often practice seven or eight hours a day.

5 Circle the best answer.

1. Rina thinks 7:00 a.m. is _____.

    a. early   **b.** the right time   **c.** late

2. Rina seldom _____.

    a. has much time on school days   **b.** gets up late   **c.** works after school

3. Rina usually _____.

    a. leaves work early   **b.** works until 6:00 p.m.   **c.** practices after school

4. Rina always eats _____ at home.

    a. breakfast   **b.** lunch   **c.** dinner

5. Rina often practices seven or eight hours a day _____.

    a. on weekends   **b.** on work days   **c.** on school days

Building Vocabulary

6 **Vocabulary Check** This is Bill's morning routine. Match the pictures and the sentences. Write the letters in the spaces.

a.

b.

c.

d.

e.

f.

_____ **1.** Bill gets up.

_____ **2.** He takes a bath.

_____ **3.** He gets dressed.

_____ **4.** He combs his hair.

_____ **5.** He eats breakfast.

_____ **6.** He brushes his teeth.

Time Expressions

at	night	**in**	the morning	**on**	weekends
	noon		the afternoon		Mondays
	six o'clock		the evening		

7 Write five true sentences about someone you know. Use time expressions with *in, on,* or *at.*

Take

8 *Take* is used in many different expressions. Complete the conversation with the correct expression from the box.

take pictures	take some aspirin
take a nap	take the bus
take a walk	take a vacation

A: It's great to be away from work. I feel so relaxed. I'm really glad we decided to **(1.)** _____.

B: Me, too. But my legs hurt from sitting on the plane for six hours. Let's **(2.)** _____ and get some fresh air.

A: OK. I'll bring the camera so we can **(3.)** _____.

[*a half hour later*]

A: Now my legs hurt and so does my head. I need to **(4.)** _____.

B: Let's **(5.)** _____ back to the hotel and you can **(6.)** _____.

Talk About It

 Work with a partner. Ask and answer questions about your morning routine. Use the expressions below.

brush (your) teeth	get up	walk the dog
get dressed	take a shower	feed the cat
take a bath	eat breakfast	read the newspaper
comb (your) hair	listen to the radio	watch the news

Example:

A: Do you take a bath in the morning?

B: No, I don't. I always take a bath at night.

A: Do you listen to the radio in the morning?

B: Yes, I do. I listen to the news.

GRAMMAR

Frequency Adverbs with the Simple Present Tense

We use frequency adverbs with the simple present tense to talk about routines. Frequency adverbs tell how often something happens.

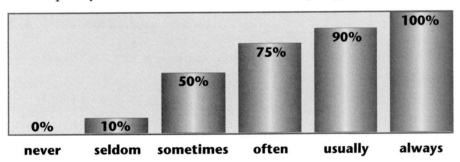

0%	10%	50%	75%	90%	100%
never	seldom	sometimes	often	usually	always

Frequency adverbs go before the main verb.

Statements
Rina **always** gets up late.
She **never** has breakfast.
Rina and her friends **seldom** have much time to practice.
Questions
Does she **often** leave work early?
Do they **always** practice after dinner?
What does she **usually** do after school?

With the verb *be*, frequency adverbs go after the verb.

Statements

Rina is **usually** on time for school.

She and her brother are **always** hungry for lunch.

Questions

Is she **always** tired at bedtime?

Is she **sometimes** late for dinner?

---

1 Think about things you do on weekends. How often do you do them?
Write a sentence for each frequency adverb in the graph on page 4.

Example:

I usually get up late on Saturdays. I never do homework on Friday evenings.

2 Unscramble these sentences. Be sure to use the correct punctuation.

Example:

you/in the morning/usually/are/hungry

Are you usually hungry in the morning?

   a. you/eat/do/breakfast/always
   b. yes,/breakfast/I/usually/eat/a big
   c. your/do/do/you/homework/when
   d. often/in the morning/it/do/I
   e. you/are/for school/ever/late
   f. never/no,/I'm/late
   g. do/what time/bed/usually/to/you/go
   h. always/I'm/asleep/by ten o'clock

 3 **Express Yourself** Talk with a partner. Ask about your partner's
weekend routine.

Example:

   A: I seldom get up early on
          Saturdays. What about you?

   B: I usually get up early on
          Saturdays. I often play
          football on Saturday
          morning.

LISTENING and SPEAKING

Listen: A Radio Interview

1 Do you know anyone who has a long-distance relationship—for example, the husband lives in one city and the wife lives in another?

STRATEGY **2** **Before You Listen** Look at the three pictures of Gilbert Burke. What information can you guess about Gilbert?

3 Listen to the interview. Then listen again. Circle the correct answers.

1. Dallas News 1 is a _____.
   a. TV channel   **b.** radio station   **c.** newspaper
2. Gilbert works _____.
   a. on weekends   **b.** at night   **c.** five days a week
3. Gilbert sees Lucy _____.
   a. in the summer   **b.** on weekends   **c.** in the summer and on weekends
4. Gilbert _____ stays up late.
   a. sometimes   **b.** never   **c.** usually
5. He's _____ asleep by eight o'clock.
   a. never   **b.** always   **c.** seldom

4 What do you think about Gilbert's lifestyle? Fill in the chart. Write four things you like about his lifestyle and four things you don't like.

Things I Like	Things I Don't Like
He's on TV.	He gets up at 3.00 a.m.

5 Work with a partner. Discuss Gilbert's lifestyle. What do you like about it? What don't you like? Do you like the same things?

Pronunciation

The –s/–es ending

We pronounce the –s ending of simple present tense verbs in three ways.
The pronunciation depends on the final sound of the verb.

/s/		/z/		/ɪz/	
start	starts	drive	drives	wash	washes
ask	asks	try	tries	close	closes
shop	shops	need	needs	watch	watches

6 Listen to and repeat each pair of verbs in the chart above. Pronounce the final sounds clearly.

7 Listen to the verbs. Which verbs have the same final sound as *dances*? Circle them. Then practice saying all the verbs.

a. brushes **d.** takes **g.** excuses

b. gets **e.** uses **h.** practices

c. exercises **f.** combs **i.** brings

Speak Out

STRATEGY **Asking Someone to Speak Louder** If you can't hear what someone is saying, you can use one of these expressions.

Would you please speak louder?	Can you please speak up?
Could you speak louder, please?	I'm sorry, I can't hear you.

8 What do you want to know about your classmates' lifestyles? With the whole class, add more questions to the chart. Then work with a partner. Ask questions and write your partner's answers.

Name:			
Do you ever ...	Yes	No	How often?
use the Internet?	☐	☐	
go to bed after midnight?	☐	☐	
play sports?	☐	☐	
listen to music?	☐	☐	
get up before 6:00 a.m.?	☐	☐	
	☐	☐	
	☐	☐	
	☐	☐	

Join another pair of students. Tell about your partner's lifestyle.

Example:

Carlos sometimes uses the Internet. He seldom goes to bed after midnight.

READING and WRITING

Read About It

 Before You Read Look at the picture. What does Vera do for a living?

Vera—On the Road Again

[1] After four years, Vera is on tour again. Born in Brazil, the twenty-nine-year-old singer grew up in Hawaii. Her unique Brazilian-Hawaiian sound made her a star at twenty-four. But her fans want concerts, and her last concert was four years ago. What happened?

[2] Vera's first album sold more than four million copies worldwide. Vera worked hard to promote it. For a year, she traveled nonstop. She did concerts and TV shows all over the world. At the end of the tour, she was sick and exhausted.

[3] Two years ago, Vera's second album sold only 350,000 copies. Vera was just married and she didn't travel to promote the album. Now there is a new album, *True Things*. Vera is traveling again—but this time she has her husband and baby with her.

[4] Touring isn't easy, but Vera says her family keeps her happy. Her husband, Kevin Goldman, thirty-five, is a university professor. He took a year off from his university to travel with Vera. Kevin plays with the baby, Max, when Vera is working. They have a nanny for the baby, so Kevin can go to Vera's concerts.

[5] Vera's routine keeps her healthy. She usually gets up at seven o'clock and meditates for an hour. She always eats breakfast with Kevin and Max. She usually has herbal tea and fruit for breakfast. Lunch is always beans, rice, and a salad. She never eats meat or drinks coffee, and she seldom eats eggs or cheese. For a special treat, she sometimes has chocolate. Before a concert or a TV show, she usually meditates again for thirty minutes. After a concert, she often sleeps for twelve hours.

[6] Today, the new album is doing well, Vera's fans are happy, and Vera has what she wants: her health, her husband, her baby—and her singing.

STRATEGY **Getting the Main Idea** Each paragraph in a reading usually has one main idea. Find the main ideas of the paragraphs you read. They will help you understand and remember the reading.

2 Match the main ideas with the paragraphs in the reading. Write the paragraph numbers in the blanks.

   a. Paragraph _____ introduces Vera.

   b. Paragraph _____ is about Vera's life today.

   c. Paragraph _____ is about Vera's family.

   d. Paragraph _____ is about Vera's routine.

   e. Paragraphs _____ and _____ are about Vera's albums.

3 Answer the questions.

   a. Where was Vera born?

   b. Where did she grow up?

   c. When was her last concert?

   d. How old is Vera?

   e. How many albums did she make?

   f. Why did Vera's first album sell so well?

   g. Why didn't her second album sell well?

   h. Why is Vera happy and healthy on this tour?

 4 **Vocabulary Check** Match the words and expressions from the reading with their meanings. Write the letters in the blanks.

_____ **1.** on the road (title); on tour (paragraph 1)	**a.** people who like her music
	b. very tired
_____ **2.** her fans (paragraph 1)	**c.** CD, tape, or record
_____ **3.** album (paragraph 2)	**d.** traveling
_____ **4.** to promote (paragraph 2)	**e.** person who takes care of babies
_____ **5.** exhausted (paragraph 2)	**f.** to make people want to buy
_____ **6.** nanny (paragraph 4)	**g.** to calm yourself, usually by sitting
_____ **7.** meditate (paragraph 5)	still and breathing quietly

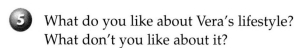

Think About It

5 What do you like about Vera's lifestyle? What don't you like about it?

6 What are some problems of being famous?

Unit 1

9

Write About It

7 **Before You Write** You want to be on *Lifestyles of Real People*, like Rina Campos on pages 1 and 2. You need to write a short letter to Rick Robinson. Write three interesting things about yourself and your lifestyle.

a. _____

b. _____

c. _____

8 **Write** Write a letter to Rick Robinson. First read Rina's letter. Begin and end your letter like Rina's.

November 17, 2000

Mr. Rick Robinson
Lifestyles of Real People
321 West 53rd Street
New York, NY 10023

Dear Mr. Robinson:

My name is Rina Campos. I always watch *Lifestyles of Real People,* and I'd like to be on the show.

I am a champion skateboarder at my high school in Chicago, Illinois. I practice skateboarding every day, usually for two hours after dinner. On weekends, I often practice eight hours a day. I also go to school from 8:15 to 3:15. Then I work in a store after school from 4:00 to 6:00. My lifestyle is very busy!

Thank you very much.

Sincerely,

Rina Campos

Rina Campos
520 Spring Street
Chicago, IL 60610

9 **Check Your Writing** Check your letter. Use the questions below. Revise your letter if necessary.

- Did you begin and end your letter like Rina's?
- Did you explain three interesting things about yourself?
- Did you use the simple present tense correctly?

PERSONALITIES

Unit **2**

Rudy: *sloppy, greedy, friendly, enthusiastic*

Diana: *ambitious, hardworking, competitive,*

Mark: *quiet, neat, kind, easygoing*

GETTING STARTED

Warm Up

1 What kind of person are you? Are you like Rudy, Diana, or Mark? Circle the words that describe you. Write three more words that describe you.

_____   _____   _____

2 Work with a partner. Tell your partner about yourself.

Example:

I'm outgoing and enthusiastic, like Rudy.
I'm also competitive, like Diana.
I'm responsible and careful, too.

What's he like?

  Listen and read.

WILL: So, little sister, tell me about your new boyfriend—Shaquil? What's he like?

KIM: Well, he's very good-looking. He dresses really well, he has a car …

WILL: Really? Where does he get the money for that?

KIM: He works for his father after school. His father owns a restaurant.

WILL: OK. What else?

KIM: Well, he's really smart, too. He gets good grades in school. He's very hardworking and responsible.

WILL: Um hum. So what does he do in his spare time?

KIM: He loves sports. He plays basketball, soccer, tennis …

WILL: Hold it! I see a problem here. You *hate* sports, Kim. Do you two have anything in common?

KIM: Of course we do.

WILL: Well, does Shaquil like going to parties? I know you can't live without parties.

KIM: Well, actually he's a little shy. He prefers staying home and watching TV. He doesn't really like meeting new people.

WILL: Does he like dancing?

KIM: He isn't a very good dancer. He gets embarrassed. But he enjoys going to museums and listening to jazz.

WILL: And you *love* dancing and you *hate* museums and jazz. You don't like the same things at all.

KIM: It's easy to criticize! But I like Shaquil, and he's never boring!

4 Circle the best answer.

1. Will and Kim are _____.

    a. brother and sister   **b.** friends   **c.** married

2. Shaquil is Kim's _____.

    a. brother   **b.** friend   **c.** new boyfriend

3. Kim says Shaquil is _____.

    a. outgoing   **b.** smart   **c.** boring

4. Shaquil feels _____ when he dances.

    a. embarrassed   **b.** tired   **c.** bored

5. Kim likes _____.

    a. going to museums   **b.** dancing   **c.** listening to jazz

6. Kim and Shaquil _____ interests in common.

    a. don't have many   **b.** have a lot of   **c.** don't want any

Building Vocabulary

 5 **Vocabulary Check** Complete the sentences with words from the box.

self-confident	enthusiastic
easygoing	messy
ambitious	smart
friendly	quiet
talented	responsible

a. Scott makes friends easily. He's really
_____.

b. Ivan always gets good grades. He's _____.

c. Roberta never gets mad about little things. She's _____.

d. Somchai doesn't talk a lot. He's very _____.

e. Tarik always knows he will do well. He's _____.

f. Edith does many things well. She's really _____.

g. Ruth never irons her clothes or puts them away. She's _____.

h. Chen always gets excited about what's happening and has a good time.
He's _____.

i. Rachel is only six, but she helps her mother a lot. She's very _____.

j. Joe wants to make a million dollars before he's thirty. He's _____.

Spare-Time Activities

6 Here are some activities people like doing in their spare time. Circle the ones you like.

a.   b.   c.   d.

e.   f.   g.   h.

7 Match the activities with the pictures in Exercise 6. Write the letters in the blanks.

1. _____ going to the movies   5. _____ shopping
2. _____ hiking   6. _____ washing the car
3. _____ listening to music   7. _____ visiting museums
4. _____ dancing   8. _____ lying around reading

Adjectives Ending in *–ing* and *–ed*

> **Adjectives** ending in *–ing* usually describe the thing or person that makes you feel a certain way.
>
> The movie was boring.
>
> **Adjectives** ending in *–ed* usually describe the emotion—how a thing or person makes you feel.
>
> I was bored.

Unit 2

8 Use the words in the box to complete the sentences. Write two more sentences. Then compare answers with a partner.

boring/bored	tiring/tired
frustrating/frustrated	embarrassing/embarrassed
relaxing/relaxed	satisfying/satisfied
frightening/frightened	exciting/excited
interesting/interested	tiring/tired

a. Dancing is _____relaxing_____.

b. Visiting a shopping mall is

_____.

c. I usually feel _____ when I get my grades in school.

d. Studying always makes me feel _____.

e. Romantic movies are _____.

f. I feel _____ when I listen to jazz.

g. _____.

h. _____.

Talk About It

9 Work with a partner. Which activities does he or she like? Ask and answer questions. Add two more activities to the chart. Write notes about your partner's answers in the chart.

Example:

A: Do you like going to the movies?

B: Yes, very much. I go to the movies about twice a month.

A: Do you enjoy hiking?

B: Not very much. It's tiring.

Do you like/enjoy … ?	Yes	No	Your Partner's Answers
a. going to the movies	☑	☐	*Goes to the movies twice a month.*
b. hiking	☐	☑	*It's tiring.*
c. listening to music	☐	☐	
d. dancing	☐	☐	
e. shopping	☐	☐	
f. washing the car	☐	☐	
g. visiting museums	☐	☐	
h. lying around reading	☐	☐	
i.	☐	☐	
j.	☐	☐	

10 Join another pair of students. Talk about your partner's spare-time activities. Use your notes from Exercise 9.

GRAMMAR

Gerunds

A gerund is the *–ing* form of the verb when it is used as a noun. Gerunds can be the subject or the object of a sentence.

Subject	Verb	
Swimming	is	good exercise.
Getting up early	isn't	much fun.

Subject	Verb	Object
Kim	enjoys	**dancing**.
Shaquil	doesn't like	**meeting** new people.

 Remember these *–ing* spelling rules:

1. For many verbs, just add *–ing*: tal**king**; play**ing**

2. For most verbs ending in **e**, take off the **e** and add *–ing*: writ**ing**; danc**ing**

3. For most words ending in one vowel and one consonant, double the last consonant before adding *–ing*: stop**ping**; run**ning**

1 Add *–ing* to the verbs. Circle the activities you enjoy doing.

a. wash _____ the dishes
b. watch _____ TV
c. write _____ letters to friends
d. shop _____ for clothes
e. speak _____ English
f. talk _____ on the phone
g. play _____ computer games
h. eat _____ out in restaurants
i. work _____ out at the gym
j. have _____ a party
k. run _____ in the park
l. ride _____ a bicycle
m. stay _____ at home
n. surf _____ the Internet
o. read _____ books
p. go _____ for a walk

2 Work with a partner. Discuss the activities you enjoy or don't enjoy doing.
Example:
A: I don't like washing the dishes. Washing the dishes is boring.
B: I like shopping for clothes. Shopping for clothes is fun.

It + Infinitive

Infinitives (*to* + verb) are often used after *it*.

It's relaxing **to listen** to music.	=	Listening to music is relaxing.
It isn't much fun **to get up** early.	=	Getting up early isn't much fun.

3 Complete the sentences with an adjective from the box. Then write new sentences with *It* + infinitive.

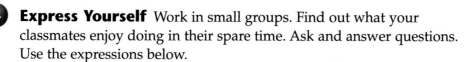

tiring	easy
boring	fun
interesting	entertaining
exciting	relaxing
frustrating	dangerous
useful	hard

   a. Going to museums is _____*fun*_____.
      It's fun to go to museums.

   b. Working out in the gym is _____.
      _____.

   c. Talking on the telephone is _____.
      _____.

   d. Going to a shopping mall is _____.   _____.

   e. Traveling to foreign countries is _____.   _____.

   f. Watching sports on TV is _____.   _____.

   g. Hiking in the mountains is _____.   _____.

   h. Sleeping late on the weekend is _____.   _____.

   i. Watching movies in English is _____.   _____.

   j. Riding a bicycle in the park is _____.   _____.

 4 **Express Yourself** Work in small groups. Find out what your classmates enjoy doing in their spare time. Ask and answer questions. Use the expressions below.

Agreeing		Disagreeing
Me, too.	Me, neither.Really?	Not me.
I do, too.	I don't either.	I don't.
So do I.	Neither do I.	Really? I do.

Example:

A: Do you like washing the dishes?

B: No, I don't.

A: Me, neither. It's boring.

C: Do you like cooking dinner?

A: Yes, I do.

C: Really? I don't. I'm a terrible cook.

LISTENING and SPEAKING

Listen: Who's Coming to Dinner?

1 Do you ever introduce different friends to each other? How do you choose who to introduce?

 2 **Before You Listen** Read the situation and study the chart in Exercise 3 on page 17. Who is speaking? What are they talking about?

🎧 **3** George and Judy asked their friend Steve to come for dinner. They want to invite another friend, too. Listen to the conversation. Fill in the chart. Put a ✓ for *likes* and an ✗ for *doesn't like*.

	Cooking	Dancing and going to clubs	Eating out in restaurants	Playing sports and talking about them
Steve				
Douglas				
Richard				
Ellen				

4 Work in small groups and discuss the following questions. Which friend would you invite to meet Steve? Why?

Pronunciation

> **Syllables**
>
> Every word has one or more beats, or syllables. For example:
>
> > **shy** has one syllable
> >
> > **greed•y** has two syllables
> >
> > **hard•work•ing** has three syllables

🎧 **5** Listen and repeat.

Kind has one syllable.	Kind.
Friendly has two syllables.	Friend•ly.
Ambitious has three syllables.	Am•bi•tious.
Self-confident has four syllables.	Self•con•fi•dent.
Enthusiastic has five syllables.	En•thu•si•as•tic.

🎧 **6** Listen to the pairs of words. Do they have the same or a different number of syllables? Check the box. Listen and repeat the words.

		Same	**Different**
a.	greedy/sloppy	☐	☐
b.	kind/quiet	☐	☐
c.	self-confident/interesting	☐	☐
d.	outgoing/easygoing	☐	☐
e.	competitive/hardworking	☐	☐
f.	easygoing/responsible	☐	☐

Unit 2

17

Speak Out

STRATEGY **Making Suggestions** You can use these expressions to make suggestions.

> **Let's** make a list of activities.
> **Why don't we** go shopping in the morning?

7 Work with a partner. You want to have fun together on Saturday. What activities do you both like to do?

- Make a list of places you want to go and things you want to do.
- Plan your day. What do you want to do first? Next? After that?

8 Join another pair of students. Share your Saturday plans.

Example:

Julie and I like shopping. We're going to get up early and go to the mall on Saturday morning. We like walking in the park, so we're going to go to the park in the afternoon. Going to the movies is another thing we enjoy. We're going to go to the movies in the evening.

READING and WRITING

Read About It

1 **Before You Read** Do you ever read the personal ads section of a newspaper? What kind of information is in the personals?

STRATEGY **Skimming** Sometimes we read something quickly. We don't try to understand every word, but we look for the general idea. This kind of reading is called skimming.

2 You are looking for a pen pal. Read the personal ads quickly. What kind of information is in every ad? Check (✓) the boxes.

| ☐ name | ☐ family information | ☐ age | ☐ birthday |
| ☐ address | ☐ job or grade in school | ☐ nationality | ☐ interests |

PEN PALS WANTED

JANE AUSTIN, 26, Australian, likes hiking, camping, swimming, eating out.

PATRICIA VALDEZ, 19, Spanish, enjoys going to the movies, making new friends, shopping.

camping

ALI OZBAL, 18, Turkish, likes reading, writing letters, seeing friends.

MARICELLA RIVERA, 20, Mexican, likes playing sports, going to clubs, listening to music, singing.

CARLOS MOLINA, 23, Ecuadorian, likes going for long walks, dancing, cooking, and driving his car.

DOLORES BETHANIA, 17, Brazilian, likes swimming, listening to music, watching soccer, speaking English.

YOSHI SATO, 21, Japanese, enjoys cooking, painting, going to museums.

ARMANDO FERNANDEZ, 25, Costa Rican, enjoys telling jokes, playing soccer, singing, playing the guitar.

MARIA CAASI, 20, Filipina, likes riding a bicycle, camping, hiking, jogging.

DANIEL STEVENS, 18, American, likes TV, movies, music, and working out.

KRISTINA PATROPOLIS, 23, Greek, enjoys going to clubs, cooking, and lying around reading.

CHUNG-PING LEE, 19, Chinese, likes playing table tennis, reading, and talking with friends.

painting

jogging

 Answer the questions.

    a. How many people enjoy reading?
    b. How many people play the guitar?
    c. How many people enjoy camping?
    d. Who enjoys playing sports and other outdoor activities?
    e. Who likes only indoor activities?

Think About It

 Who would you like as a pen pal? Why? What things do you have in common with this person?

Write About It

5 **Before You Write** Renata Scatena wrote to Dolores Bethania. Here is her letter. Did she choose a good pen pal? Why or why not?

> 25 Via Marconi
> Milan, Italy
>
> March 9, 2000
>
> Dear Dolores,
>
>   Hello! My name is Renata Scatena. I'm a student and I'm 16 years old. I live in Milan with my parents and my two brothers. I like writing in English, and I'd like you to be my pen pal.
>   I know you enjoy listening to music. I like pop music. My favorite singer is Celine Dion. Who is your favorite singer? I like sports, too. I think it's fun to go swimming and hiking. I often go hiking with my brothers. I'm a serious person and I enjoy going to school. Do you like school? What's your favorite class?
>   I love writing letters in English. Do you want to be my pen pal? Please write to me soon.
>
> Yours truly,
>
> *Renata Scatena*
>
> Renata Scatena

6 **Write** Write a letter to one of the people in the newspaper ads on pages 18 and 19. Tell about three things that you like to do in your spare time. Write one or two sentences about each thing you like to do. Begin and end your letter like Renata's letter.

 7 **Check Your Writing** Reread your letter. Answer the questions below. Then revise your letter as necessary.

- Did you tell about two things you like to do in your spare time?
- Did you begin and end your letter like Renata's?
- Did you use gerunds and infinitives correctly?

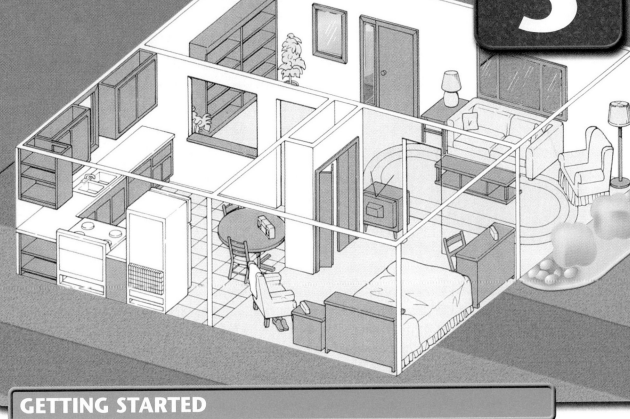

GETTING STARTED

Warm Up

1 Write the correct words on the lines.

above	under
behind	in front of
between	across from
next to	in the corner
on	

a. There's a radio _____ the table.

b. The rug is _____ the floor in the living room.

c. There's a table _____ the couch.

d. There's a desk _____ the closet.

e. The bookcase is _____ two plants.

f. The tall lamp is _____ the big chair.

g. The stove is _____ the refrigerator and the sink.

h. The bed is _____ of the bedroom.

i. There's a pair of shoes _____ the chair in the bedroom.

j. The cupboards are _____ the sink and the counter.

2 Work with a partner. Ask and answer questions about the picture above.

Example:

A: Where's the stove?

B: It's next to the refrigerator.

It's perfect!

 3 Eve and Joe Bradley are talking with a sales agent about a new house. Listen and read.

AGENT: How many bedrooms will you need?

JOE: We'll need three. One for us, one for our son, and one for my grandmother. We need one bedroom downstairs so my grandmother won't have to climb the stairs.

AGENT: I think you're going to like this plan. This house has a bedroom and a bathroom downstairs.

EVE: That's good, but look at the kitchen, Joe. It's too small. Our stove and refrigerator will fit here, but it isn't big enough for a table and chairs.

AGENT: But there's a dining room next to the kitchen. You can eat there.

EVE: I prefer eating in the kitchen most of the time. It's easier with a small child.

AGENT: Here's a plan with a bigger kitchen. And here are some photographs.

EVE: I like the sink and the counters, and there are two windows and lots of cupboards.

JOE: But there are only two bedrooms. We need three.

EVE: No, look, Joe. There's a TV room downstairs. We won't need a TV room. It'll make a great bedroom for your grandmother. But there's no closet. Can you add a closet?

AGENT: No problem. We'll add one.

JOE: Great! But the downstairs bathroom doesn't have a shower. Grandma will have to go upstairs to take a shower.

AGENT: No, she won't. We'll make the bathroom bigger. We can add a shower across from the sink. What do you think?

EVE: Grandma's going to love it. Oh, and look! There's a laundry room here between the kitchen and the garage. It's perfect!

4 Answer the questions.

    a. How many people are going to live in the house?

    b. Why doesn't Eve like the plan for the first house?

    c. Does Eve like the kitchen in the second plan? Why or why not?

    d. Will the downstairs bathroom have a shower? Why or why not?

Building Vocabulary

 5 **Vocabulary Check** Complete the sentences. Write the letters on the lines.

1. _____ I read and watch TV	**a.** in the laundry room.
2. _____ They keep their car	**b.** in the bedroom.
3. _____ He cooks dinner	**c.** on the stove.
4. _____ We eat dinner	**d.** in the living room.
5. _____ I sleep	**e.** in the bathroom.
6. _____ She puts dishes	**f.** in the garage.
7. _____ They keep food	**g.** in the dishwasher.
8. _____ You wash and dry clothes	**h.** in the closet.
9. _____ We take a shower	**i.** in the dining room.
10. _____ I keep my clothes	**j.** in the refrigerator.

Things in a House

Appliances	**Furniture**		**Other Household Items**	
dishwasher	bed	desk	lamp	counter
refrigerator	bookcase	dresser	rug	sink
stove	chair	table	bathtub	closet
washer/dryer	couch		cupboard	

6 Work in groups. What things go in the rooms below? Make a list. Use the words from the box above and your own words. Some things can go in more than one room. Use a separate piece of paper. Compare lists with another group.

Living room	Kitchen	Bedroom	Bathroom	Dining room

Prepositions of Place: *in, on, at*

We use *in* with the names of cities, countries, continents, and mountain ranges.

> My grandfather lives **in** Cairo. Cairo is **in** Egypt. Egypt is **in** Africa.
>
> Quito is a city **in** the Andes. The Andes are **in** South America.

We also use *in* to mean inside a place or building.

> Eve and Joe are **in** the house. | Juan's brother is sick. He's **in** the hospital.
> Let's go rollerblading **in** the park. | The car is **in** the garage.

We use *on* with floors of a building, avenues, and streets.

> I live **on** the first floor of a tall apartment building.
> Joe works **on** Second Avenue.

We use *at* to show a general location or a specific street address.

General Location	Specific Address
Ron is **at** work.	His office is **at** 10 Bank Street.
The concert is **at** the library.	The library is **at** 5th Avenue and 42nd Street.
We'll meet you **at** the theater.	The theater is **at** 1221 Broadway.

7 Joe and his father are talking on the phone. Complete the conversation with *in, on,* or *at.*

JOE: Dad, we just bought a house! It's **(1.)** _____ Park Lane **(2.)** _____ Pleasantville.

DAD: Pleasantville?

JOE: You know, it's **(3.)** _____ the Palisades Mountains, near Jamestown. The house is **(4.)** _____ 7 Park Lane. It has a bedroom **(5.)** _____ the first floor for Grandma.

DAD: That's great news, Joe. Listen, where are you now?

JOE: I'm **(6.)** _____ the house. Eve and I are talking to the sales agent.

DAD: I'm **(7.)** _____ work, so I can't talk now. But I'll meet you for dinner **(8.)** _____ the seafood restaurant **(9.)** _____ Spring Street at 6:30. We can talk then.

JOE: OK. It's so hot today. Let's meet **(10.)** _____ the restaurant. It'll be cooler there.

DAD: OK. See you later!

Talk About It

8 Work with a partner. Talk about things in your home. What do you have? Where?

Example:

I have a computer in my bedroom.
It's on the table next to the window.

GRAMMAR

The Future Tense with *Will*

We use *will* + verb to talk about the future.

Affirmative Statement	Negative Statement
I **will make** the bathroom bigger.	We **won't need** a TV room.
Yes/No Question	**Short Answers**
Will the refrigerator **fit** in the kitchen?	Yes, it **will**./No, it **won't**.
Information Question	**Answer**
How many bedrooms **will** you **need**?	We'**ll need** three.

 note (we) will = (we)'ll   will + not = won't

The Future with *Be going to*

We use *be going to* + verb to talk about future plans.

> My grandmother **is going to live** with us.
>
> Eve and Joe **are going to talk** to the sales agent tonight.

note *Will* and *be going to* often have the same meaning.

They will need three bedrooms. = They are going to need three bedrooms.

1 Complete the conversation with *will* or *am/is/are*. Then practice it with a partner.

EVE: We **(1.)** _____ going to build a new house.

SUE: Really? How big **(2.)** _____ it be?

EVE: It **(3.)** _____ going to have nine rooms plus a hall and a garage. I think I **(4.)** _____ paint the kitchen yellow.

SUE: It sounds like it **(5.)** _____ going to be beautiful.

EVE: Thanks. We **(6.)** _____ going to get some furniture from my parents, too. I can't wait! The house **(7.)** _____ be so nice to live in.

2 Complete the conversation. If there is a future plan, use *am/am not going to*. If there isn't a plan, use *will/won't*.

BOB: Do you want to go shopping with me?

TOM: Sure. Maybe I **(1.)** _____ buy a new lamp for my desk.

BOB: Oh, I **(2.)** _____ go to the furniture store. I need a new jacket. I **(3.)** _____ look in the clothing store. I don't think we **(4.)** _____ have time to go to the furniture store, too.

TOM: Oh. Well, I really hate shopping for clothing. I guess I **(5.)** _____ go with you after all. Thanks anyway.

Too and Not ... enough with Adjectives

We use *too* + adjective to show that something is not possible.

> We can't live in this house. Our family is **too big**.
>
> We want a bigger house, but we're **too poor**.

Not + adjective + *enough*
also shows that something
is not possible.

> We can't live in this house. It is**n't big enough**.
>
> We want a bigger house, but we are**n't rich enough**.

3 Look at the pictures. Each person wants to do something but can't. Complete
the sentences. Use *too* or *not ... enough* and the adjective in parentheses.

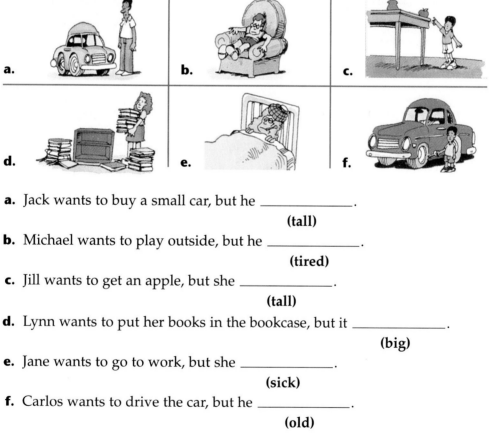

a.

b.

c.

d.

e.

f.

a. Jack wants to buy a small car, but he _____.
(tall)

b. Michael wants to play outside, but he _____.
(tired)

c. Jill wants to get an apple, but she _____.
(tall)

d. Lynn wants to put her books in the bookcase, but it _____.
(big)

e. Jane wants to go to work, but she _____.
(sick)

f. Carlos wants to drive the car, but he _____.
(old)

4 Write two sentences about yourself with *too* + adjective. Write two sentences
with *not* + adjective + *enough*. Then read your sentences to a partner.

5 **Express Yourself** Work with a partner. Discuss your plans for the weekend. Talk about what you are going to do. Use *too* and *not … enough*.

Example:

This Saturday, I'm going to see the new Steven Spielberg movie at the Cineplex. I hope the lines aren't too long and the tickets aren't too expensive. On Sunday, I'm going to play football with my friends. We're going to play in the park.

LISTENING and SPEAKING

Listen: "Welcome to the White House!"

The White House

The Oval Office

1 What do you know about the White House? Would you like to take a tour of the White House? What do you think you would see there?

STRATEGY **2** **Before You Listen** Look at the pictures and the title above. What do you think the listening will be about? What kind of information do you think you will hear?

  3 Study the chart. Listen to the tour guide. Then check (✓) the rooms and furniture on the tour.

Rooms on the Tour	Furniture on the Tour
☐ Red Room	☐ Portrait of President Lincoln
☐ Blue Room	☐ Portrait of Mrs. Lincoln
☐ Family Dining Room	☐ Portrait of President Washington
☐ State Dining Room	☐ French dining room table
☐ East Room	☐ President Washington's table
☐ East Wing	☐ *Resolute* desk
☐ Lincoln Bedroom	☐ Lincoln desk
☐ Oval Office	☐ Lincoln bed

Pronunciation

Stressed Syllables

In English, one syllable is stressed more than the others.
Often, the first syllable is stressed:

> báthtub   cábinet   télevision

Sometimes the second syllable is stressed:

> garáge   muséum   appliánces

4   Listen to and repeat the words above.

5   Listen to these words. Notice the stress. Which syllable is stressed?
Check (✓) the correct box for each word.

	First Syllable	Second Syllable
a. dishwasher	☐	☐
b. radio	☐	☐
c. TV	☐	☐
d. television	☐	☐
e. electric	☐	☐
f. library	☐	☐
g. laundry	☐	☐
h. exhibit	☐	☐
i. refrigerator	☐	☐
j. toilet	☐	☐

6   Now listen again and repeat the words.

Speak Out

STRATEGY **Taking Turns** It is polite to take turns in conversation.

Asking whose turn it is:	Telling someone it is his or her turn:
Whose turn is it?	It's your turn, Raquel.
Who's next?	You're next, Luis.

7   Work in small groups. Talk about an interesting or beautiful house
you know. It can be a friend's or family member's house. Or it can be
a historic place or museum. Where is it? After you talk, people in your
group can ask questions. Take turns.

Example:

A: The Royal Pavilion in Brighton is really interesting. From the outside, it looks like a palace in India. The furniture and paintings inside are Chinese. It has many large rooms on two floors. It has beautiful gardens outside.

B: Where is Brighton?

A: It's in England. It's a city on the sea, south of London.

READING and WRITING

Read About It

1 **Before You Read** In your country, do college students usually live at home? What are the advantages and disadvantages of living at home?

STRATEGY **Scanning** When you get a letter, you sometimes read it quickly to find specific information. This is called scanning.

2 Steven is going to college in another city. He's looking for an apartment. He wrote a letter to his parents. Scan Steven's letter. Find the answers to these questions.

a. Did Steven find an apartment?   **c.** Does he have a roommate?

b. How much is the rent?   **d.** Who is it?

Dear Mom and Dad,

[1] I got an apartment! It's $600 a month, so I need a roommate. I'm going to share it with Michael Gray. We'll split the rent 50-50. Do you remember him? He's quiet, and I think I'll like living with him.

[2] The apartment has one bedroom, a big living room that will double as a bedroom, and a tiny kitchen. There's a bathroom, too, with a shower. I'm going to sleep in the living room for now, but we'll change places in December. Michael will have his TV and stereo in the bedroom and mine will be in the living room, so we won't bother each other too much.

[3] We went to a second-hand furniture store and bought some things. I got a bed, a dresser, and a desk for $130. We also got a couch and a table with three chairs. They cost $150, but my half was only $75. Can I have the rug from my room at home and the chair and my two lamps? I'll be home on the 31st to pick up my stuff.

[4] Say hi to Vicki and Kathy for me. See you soon!

Love,
Steven

Vocabulary Check Match the words and expressions with their meanings. Write the letters next to the numbers.

—— **1.** got (paragraphs 1, 3)

—— **2.** roommate (paragraph 1)

—— **3.** to share (paragraph 1)

—— **4.** to split 50-50 (paragraph 1)

—— **5.** to double as (paragraph 2)

—— **6.** tiny (paragraph 2)

—— **7.** to bother (paragraph 2)

—— **8.** second-hand (paragraph 3)

—— **9.** to pick up (paragraph 3)

—— **10.** stuff (paragraph 3)

a. to live in the same place with someone

b. things

c. found; bought

d. a person you live with, not a relative

e. used, not new

f. to take

g. to disturb

h. very small

i. to also be used as

j. to pay half

Think About it

 What do you like about Steven's apartment? What don't you like about it?

  Would you like to have a roommate? Why or why not?

Write About It

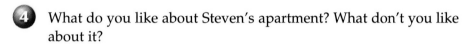 **Before You Write** You just found a new apartment or house. Answer these questions.

a. Where is it?

b. How much is it going to cost? (How much is the rent?)

c. When will you move?

d. How many bedrooms, bathrooms, and other rooms does it have?

e. What furniture will you buy? Make a list.

 Write Write a letter to your best friend. Follow the same form as Steven's letter on page 29, but use your own information. In paragraph 1, answer questions a.–c. from Exercise 6. In paragraph 2, answer question d. Answer question e. in paragraph 3. Write a short closing paragraph similar to Steven's.

 Check Your Writing Use the questions below to check your writing. Revise your letter if necessary.

- Did you follow the form of Steven's letter?
- Did you use *will* and *be going to* correctly?
- Is your spelling correct?

Unit 3

1 Complete the reading with the correct form of the verb in parentheses. Use the simple present or the future tense with *be going to*.

Lucy Burke **(1. be)** _____ a dancer with the New York Metro Ballet. She always **(2. get up)** _____ at eight o'clock and **(3. eat)** _____ a small breakfast. Lucy and the other dancers **(4. practice)** _____ in the morning. In the afternoon, Lucy usually **(5. have)** _____ some free time. At about six o'clock, she **(6. go)** _____ to the theater. The performance **(7. start)** _____ at eight o'clock.

Tomorrow, Lucy and the other dancers **(8. fly)** _____ to Dallas. They **(9. be)** _____ in Dallas for twelve weeks. In Dallas, Lucy **(10. dance)** _____ in *Swan Lake* for the first time.

2 Complete the conversation with the words in parentheses. For future plans, use the correct form of *be going to*. If there isn't a plan, use the correct form of *will*.

ANGIE: **(1. I/go)** _____ to the movies tonight. Do you want to come with me?

LEON: What **(2. you/see)** _____?

ANGIE: *Smart Money*.

LEON: Oh, **(3. I/see)** _____ that next Saturday. I guess **(4. I/go)** _____ with you. Sorry.

ANGIE: Well, maybe **(5. I/wait)** _____ and see it later. **(6. I/have)** _____ dinner with Jerry on Friday. Maybe **(7. we/see)** _____ *Smart Money* on Friday, too.

LEON: Great! Then how about that new Brazilian movie for tonight? **(8. My teacher/talk)** _____ about it in class on Monday.

ANGIE: Sure. That sounds fine.

3 Rewrite these sentences with a gerund.

a. It's wonderful to swim in the sea. _____

b. It's exciting to travel. _____

c. It isn't fun to live alone. _____

Rewrite these sentences with an infinitive.

a. Making new friends is easy. _____

b. Bicycling in the country is great. _____

c. Waiting for people is boring. _____

4 Read the graph about Kim's activities. Write sentences with frequency adverbs. Use a separate piece of paper.

Kim's Activities

a. eats dinner with her family

b. is in bed at 11:00 p.m.

c. studies with her boyfriend

d. is bored in museums

e. plays sports

f. is late for school

0%   50%   100%

5 Complete the sentences with *in*, *on*, or *at*.

a. The museum is closed _____ Mondays.

b. I use a computer _____ work.

c. My aunt and uncle live _____ Washington, D.C.

d. We usually phone our relatives _____ the weekend.

e. Allen is _____ the hospital. He's very sick.

f. I'm often busy _____ the evening.

g. Let's meet _____ six o'clock.

h. Aziz is _____ the backyard.

i. My office is _____ the twenty-third floor.

Vocabulary Review

above	nationality
furniture	behind
between	interests
appliances	personality
garage	responsible

a. They asked my name, age, and _____.

b. The kitchen has new _____, including the stove and refrigerator.

c. There's a closet _____ the kitchen and the TV room.

d. The living room is on the first floor. My bedroom is on the second floor, _____ the living room.

e. All of our _____ is old. We're going to buy a new sofa.

f. My wife never puts the car in the _____.

g. She's smart and fun and very kind. She has a great _____.

h. I was _____ the door so she didn't see me.

i. She has many _____. She enjoys sports, reading, and making new friends.

j. Katya is a _____ worker. She never misses a day of work.

GETTING STARTED

Warm Up

1. Think of a job you would like and a job you would not like. What kind of personality do you need for each job? Complete the chart below. Use some of the words that describe personality in Exercise 5 on page 13 of Unit 2.

I want to be:	I don't want to be:
_____	_____
Personality:	Personality:
_____	_____
_____	_____

2. Work with a partner. Talk about the jobs and personalities you wrote in the chart above.

Example:

A: What do you want to be?

B: I want to be a computer programmer.

A: What kind of personality do computer programmers need?

B: They need to be smart, hardworking, and careful.

The job is yours.

 3 Listen and read.

MR. RODRIGUEZ:	I need an assistant in the shop and the greenhouse. It's three afternoons a week—Monday, Wednesday, and Thursday. The job is yours. Can you start tomorrow?
MATTHEW:	Yes, I can. What time do I have to be here? And what do I have to do?
MR. RODRIGUEZ:	You have to be here at three o'clock. From three until six, you help the customers. You get plants for them.
MATTHEW:	OK. Do I have to learn the names of all the plants?
MR. RODRIGUEZ:	You can, but you don't have to. Each plant has its name on it.
MATTHEW:	That's good. What time does the shop close?
MR. RODRIGUEZ:	We close at six o'clock. After we close, you have to water some of the plants. That takes an hour. You have to be careful when you water them. You can't give them too much water. I'll show you tomorrow. You also have to clean up the shop.
MATTHEW:	Clean up the shop?
MR. RODRIGUEZ:	Yes, that takes an hour, too. Before you go home, you sweep the floors and take out the garbage. The shop has to be ready for business when we open in the morning. Any other questions?
MATTHEW:	Uh, yeah. How much money will I make?
MR. RODRIGUEZ:	The pay is thirty dollars a day.
MATTHEW:	That's fine. Thanks, Mr. Rodriguez. I'll see you tomorrow.
MR. RODRIGUEZ:	You're welcome. See you at three.

4 Circle the correct answer.

1. Matthew is going to work in _____.

    a. a shop   **b.** a greenhouse   **c.** a shop and a greenhouse

2. When the shop is open, Matthew has to _____.

    a. sweep the floors   **b.** get plants for the customers   **c.** water the plants

3. Matthew has to clean up the shop _____.

    a. after he waters the plants   **b.** before the shop closes   **c.** before the shop opens

4. Matthew has to work from about 3:00 p.m. to _____.

    a. 6:00 p.m.   **b.** 7:00 p.m.   **c.** 8:00 p.m.

5. Matthew is going to make ninety dollars _____.

    a. a day   **b.** a week   **c.** a month

Building Vocabulary
Occupations

a. artist

b. biologist

c. waiter/waitress

d. travel agent

e. police officer

f. photographer

g. engineer

h. gardener

 5 **Vocabulary Check** Match the occupations above with the descriptions. Write the correct letter in the blank.

_____ **1.** She studies plants and animals. She observes many living things.

_____ **2.** He takes care of grass, trees, and flowers.

_____ **3.** He paints pictures and sells them. His paintings are colorful.

_____ **4.** He works for the city. Sometimes his job is dangerous.

_____ **5.** She takes photographs. Her pictures are in newspapers and magazines.

_____ **6.** He plans trips for people. His clients enjoy their travels.

_____ **7.** She designs new bridges. Her bridges are safe.

_____ **8.** They work in a restaurant. They serve food to customers.

6 Match each word with one that has a similar meaning. Write the correct letter in the blank.

_____ **1.** safe   **a.** designs

_____ **2.** studies   **b.** client

_____ **3.** plans   **c.** photographs

_____ **4.** customer   **d.** observes

_____ **5.** pictures   **e.** not dangerous

_____ **6.** trips   **f.** travels

Do and *Make*

Do usually means "perform."

I can **do** many things.	Did he **do** the work?
I can **do** the job.	She **did** well on the test.

Make usually means "create," "build," or "put together."

I can **make** many things.	Did you **make** the salad?
I can **make** a dress.	He **made** a graph.

Do and *make* are also used in many common expressions in English.

do the laundry	make friends
do the housework	make an appointment
do the shopping	make a mistake
do (your) best	make money
do (me) a favor	make a decision
_____	_____
_____	_____

7 Work with a partner. Discuss the meanings of the expressions above. Can you think of other expressions with *do* or *make*? Add them to the list.

8 Write six sentences about yourself. Use three expressions with *do* and three with *make*.

Talk About It

9 Work with a partner. Read your sentences from Exercise 8 to your partner. Ask your partner a question about each of his or her sentences.

Example:

A: I made a mistake yesterday.

B: What did you do?

A: I didn't call my niece. It was her birthday.

GRAMMAR

Before, After, and *When*

We use the words *before, after,* and *when* to introduce time clauses. When they are in the first clause, we use a comma between the two clauses.

First Clause	Second Clause
Before Larry designs a house,	he talks with his client.
Larry talks with his client	**before** he designs a house.
After Larry designs the house,	he builds it.
Larry builds the house	**after** he designs it.
When Larry builds the house,	he follows the plans.
Larry follows the plans	**when** he builds the house.

 A clause is a group of words that has a subject and a verb.

1 Look at the conversation on page 34. Find four sentences with time clauses with *before, after,* or *when*. Write them below. Use commas where necessary.

a. _____ .

b. _____ .

c. _____ .

d. _____ .

2 Look at the grammar box above. Answer the questions about Larry. Write complete sentences.

a. What does Larry do first?   He _____ .

b. What does he do next?   He _____ .

c. What does he do last?   He _____

       and _____ .

Unit 4

37

3 Work with a partner. Ask and answer questions about Larry's schedule. Use the words below.

Larry's Typical Workday

8:30 a.m.	has coffee/checks his e-mail and voice mail
8:45 a.m.	answers his e-mail
9:15 a.m.	phones clients
10:00 a.m.	has a meeting with his boss
11:00 a.m.	works on new designs
1:30 p.m.	has lunch/talks with the other architects
2:30 p.m.	goes to the new building
3:30 p.m.	checks the building/makes notes
5:00 p.m.	corrects the plans
6:00 p.m.	goes home

a. when/check his e-mail
b. after/have coffee
c. after/phones clients
d. before/have lunch
e. when/have lunch
f. after/have lunch
g. when/make notes
h. after/correct the plans

Example:

A: What does Larry do when he checks his e-mail and voice mail?

B: When he checks his e-mail and voice mail, he has coffee.

Have to/Has to

We use *have to* or *has to* + verb to express necessity.

Affirmative Statements	Negative Statements
Matthew **has to water** the plants.	He **doesn't have to do** the dishes.
We **have to study** tonight.	They **don't have to study** tonight.

Yes/No Questions	Short Answers
Do you **have to sweep** the floors?	Yes, I **do**./No, I **don't**.
Does she **have to help** customers?	Yes, she **does**./No, she **doesn't**.

Information Questions	Possible Answers
What **does** Matt **have to do** now?	He **has to do** his homework now.
Where **do** you **have to go**?	I **have to go** to work.

4 a. With the whole class, add three occupations to the list below.

travel agent	waiter	artist	dentist	_____
doctor	nurse	flight attendant	photographer	_____
teacher	gardener	police officer	salesperson	_____

b. Work in small groups. What do the people in part **a.** have to do on their jobs? Ask and answer questions. Use the activities in the box and your own ideas.

work with people	work inside
work at home	work at night
use special equipment	talk on the phone a lot
write a lot	help people
work alone	work outside
work during the day	travel a lot
be creative	tell people what to do
sell things	design things
	wear a uniform

Example:

A: What does a biologist have to do?

B: A biologist has to work outside or in a laboratory. Sometimes she has to use a microscope.

C: She has to read and write a lot, too.

5 On a separate piece of paper, write three things you have to do and three you don't have to do at home and at school.

6 **Express Yourself** Work with a partner. Ask and answer questions about what you have to do at school or home.

Example:

A: Do you have to study grammar at school?

B: Yes, I do. Do you have to do the dishes at home?

A: No, I don't.

LISTENING and SPEAKING

Listen: Career Counseling

1 What kind of job do you want to have? Why?

STRATEGY **2** **Before You Listen** Look at the picture, the title above, and the chart below in Exercise 3. What do you think the people are talking about?

3 Study the chart. Then listen to the conversation between Laura and Ted. They talk about eleven different careers. Check (✓) them.

☐ actor	☐ dentist	☐ lawyer	☐ police officer
☐ architect	☐ doctor	☐ manager	☐ salesperson
☐ artist	☐ engineer	☐ musician	☐ social worker
☐ biologist	☐ flight attendant	☐ nurse	☐ teacher
☐ dancer	☐ interior designer	☐ photographer	☐ travel agent

4 What kind of person is Laura? What does she want in life? Study the chart. Then listen and check (✓) the correct expressions.

Laura is ...	Laura wants ...
☐ friendly	☐ to work with other people
☐ artistic	☐ to work alone
☐ creative	☐ to help other people
☐ musical	☐ a good job
☐ outgoing	☐ a nice life
☐ shy	☐ to go to graduate school
☐ visual	☐ to be well paid

Pronunciation

Stressed Words

In spoken English, some words in a sentence are stressed more than others. They are pronounced louder and longer. These stressed words usually give the most important information in the sentence.

He **wants** an **exciting job**.

5 Each sentence below has three stressed words. Listen to these sentences and notice the stressed words.

 a. She **has** to **learn** the **names**.
 b. **Where** do you **have** to **go**?
 c. Does she **have** to **help** the **customers**?
 d. He **doesn't** have to **water** the **plants**.

6 Listen again and repeat the sentences. Stress the correct words.

Speak Out

STRATEGY **Responding to Guesses** When you want to say a guess is correct or incorrect, you can use these expressions.

| Yes, that's right. | You got it. | No, that's wrong. | No way. |

7 Work with a partner. Look at the list of jobs and the list of things people do on their jobs on pages 38–39. Take turns. Student A chooses a job. Student B asks *yes/no* questions to guess the job.

Example:

A: Is your job dangerous? 　　**A:** Are you a waiter?

B: No. 　　**B:** No, that's wrong.

A: Do you work with people? 　　**A:** Are you a salesperson?

B: Yes, I do. 　　**B:** You got it!

Read About It

1 **Before You Read** Look at the pictures. Where does this scientist work? What do you think she does?

Sylvia Earle's Deep-Water Career

[1] Dr. Sylvia Earle is probably the most famous marine biologist in the world today. In her work, she goes under the ocean and observes the plants and animals there. When she goes into the water, she has two questions: "How deep can I go?" and "How long can I stay?" In her career, she has faced danger in order to see more of the world under water.

[2] As a child, Sylvia Earle swam and watched the fish swimming below her. In college, she learned to scuba dive. With scuba gear, she went down to 196 feet (60 meters). She could stay there only a short time, and she wanted to stay down longer.

[3] After she finished graduate school, Dr. Earle spent two weeks under the sea. She lived with other scientists in an "apartment house" 49 feet (15 meters) down. With scuba gear, she went outside for many hours at a time. She learned many new things about the plants and animals there. It was a big step for marine biology.

[4] Almost ten years later, Dr. Earle got a chance to go much deeper under the sea. To do this, she had to put on a special diving suit that weighed 1,205 pounds (450 kilograms). Next, she took a "taxi," a small submarine, to the bottom. Then, for more than two hours, she walked on the ocean floor—1,246 feet (380 meters) down. This walk is still a record.

[5] A few years ago, Dr. Earle went down to 3,280 feet (1,000 meters) in a special submarine. But the deepest part of the ocean is 36,089 feet (11,000 meters). That is where Sylvia Earle wants to go. She needs a new kind of submarine that can go there and stay there for a long time. When it is ready, she will be able to study the deepest part of the ocean.

STRATEGY **Sequencing** To help remember the events in an article, put them in the correct order.

2 Number the statements 1–5 in the correct order.

_____ **a.** She went down to 1,246 feet.

_____ **b.** She learned to scuba dive.

_____ **c.** She went down to 3,280 feet.

_____ **d.** She stayed under the ocean for two weeks.

_____ **e.** She went to graduate school.

Vocabulary Check Look at the word box.
Make two lists of words with similar meanings.

below	see	deep	under
down	study	observe	watch

below _____ _____   observe _____ _____

_____ _____   _____ _____

Think About It

4 Why do you think Sylvia Earle wants to go deeper under the ocean
and stay down longer?

5 Would you enjoy Dr. Earle's job? Why or why not?

Write About It

 6 **Before You Write** Scientists,
like Dr. Earle, take notes on what
they observe. Go to a park, mall,
or other place and observe people
for several minutes. Take notes.
Write the date, the place, the
people, and what happens.

> Date: October 30
> Place: Greens Park
> Subjects: two boys, woman and a dog
> 10:30   two boys playing with a ball
> 10:33   young woman walking a brown dog
> 10:34   dog takes ball and runs away; boys
>   run after dog

7 **Write** Write a paragraph about your observations. Use the past
tense. Use this sample as a model.

> At ten-thirty on Saturday morning, two boys played with a ball in Greens
> Park. A young woman walked her dog. When the dog saw the boys, it ran over and
> took their ball. The dog ran away with the ball, and the boys ran after it. Soon
> the dog and the boys played together. After they played for a few minutes, the
> boys were tired. They lay down on the grass to rest. When the woman called the
> dog, it ran over to her, and they walked away.

  8 **Check Your Writing** Reread your paragraph carefully.
Use the questions below and revise as necessary.

- Did you use the simple past tense correctly?
- Did you use *when, after,* or *before* correctly?
- Is your spelling correct?

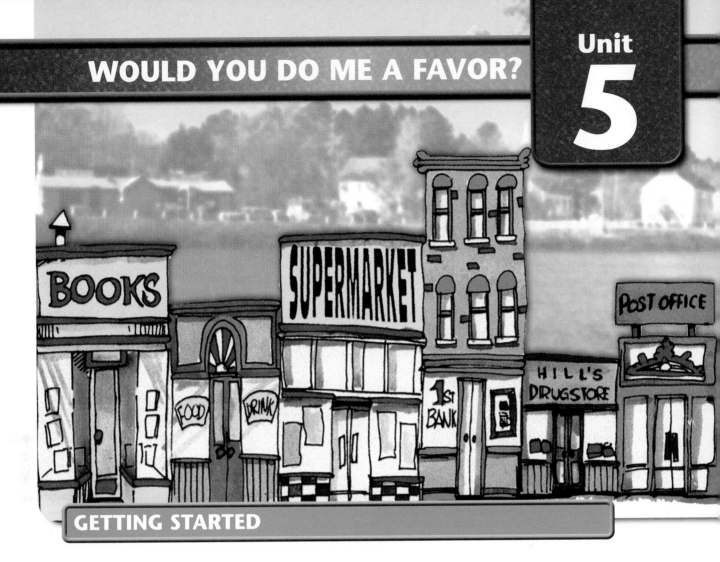

GETTING STARTED

Warm Up

 1 Look at the picture. What can you do in each building? Work with a partner. Take turns asking your partner to do you a favor in each of the buildings.

Example:

A: I can't go to the bank today. Could you deposit my check for me?

B: Sure, no problem.

Would you mind doing me a really big favor?

 2 Listen and read.

JAMES: Hey, Alan. What's the matter? You look stressed out.

ALAN: I am *totally* stressed out! I have to get ready for the party, and I also have to study for my test. Listen, would you mind doing me a really big favor? Could you do some errands for me?

JAMES: Sure. It's my day off. What do you need me to do?

ALAN: Oh, great. Thanks, James. OK, could you go to the bank and deposit my check?

JAMES: No problem. Give me the check, and I'll go to the bank.

ALAN: Now, do you remember my neighbor Janice Jackson? She bought napkins and paper plates for me at the supermarket. She also got some sodas for me. Would you mind picking them up and taking them to my apartment? And could you put the sodas in the refrigerator?

JAMES: OK. What else?

ALAN: Let me think … Oh, yeah. Could you call Pizza Kitchen for me and order four large cheese pizzas? I'll pick them up after my test.

JAMES: Sure. Would you please tell me one thing? Why did you plan a party for the same day as your test?

ALAN: Didn't I tell you? It's a surprise party for Carmela. Today's her birthday.

JAMES: Uh-huh! Now I get it. So what's in this box? Is this Carmela's present? Do you want me to give it to her?

ALAN: No, thanks! She's my girlfriend. I'll give it to her myself.

3 Answer these questions.

- **a.** What is James going to do for Alan?
- **b.** What did Janice Jackson do for Alan?
- **c.** Where does James have to go?
- **d.** What place does he have to telephone?
- **e.** What will Alan do after his test?
- **f.** Who is Carmela?
- **g.** What is the reason for the party?
- **h.** Do you think Alan invited James to the party?

Building Vocabulary

4 **Vocabulary Check** Complete each paragraph with words from the box. Use the correct form of the verb.

buy	make
call	take
cash	write
do	

Paul is a secretary. He has to **(1.)** _____ a lot of personal errands for his boss. He has to **(2.)** _____ checks for his boss at the bank. He has to **(3.)** _____ presents for his boss to give to people. He also **(4.)** _____ all his boss's appointments. He **(5.)** _____ invitations for his boss. He **(6.)** _____ his boss's suits to the cleaners. He even has to **(7.)** _____ his boss's wife when the boss is going to get home late. Paul is looking for a new job.

Marie works at the post office. Mail carriers and customers **(8.)** _____ letters and packages to her. She **(9.)** _____ them to people in other cities. When packages come from other cities, she **(10.)** _____ them to people here. Marie **(11.)** _____ stamps to customers, too. She always **(12.)** _____ "thank you" to her customers.

sell	bring
give	send
say	

Could you ... ? Would you ... ?

When you want someone to do something for you, you can use a polite request. A polite request is often a question.

> Could you (please) go to the post office for me?
>
> Would you (please) bring me some coffee?
>
> Would you mind giving this to Carol?

5 Find seven polite requests in the conversation on pages 43 and 44. Underline them. How many use _Could you_ ... ? _Would you_ ... ? or _Would you mind_ ... ? How many use _please_?

Talk About It

6 Work with a partner. Take turns asking your partner for help. Use polite requests. Add three more errands to the list.

a. buy me a newspaper

b. cash a check for me

c. buy some flowers for me

d. send this package to Gloria

e. mail these letters for me

f. do me a favor

g. take this letter to Kareem for me

h. do some errands for me

i. order a pizza for me

j. bring me a soda

Example:

A: Would you mind getting me the newspaper?

B: Sure. No problem.

GRAMMAR

Direct and Indirect Objects

Some verbs have two objects: a direct object and an indirect object. When the direct object is first, use _to_ or _for_ before the indirect object.

	Verb	Direct Object	To/For	Indirect Object
Alex	gave	flowers	**to**	Jane.
Laura	bought	a car	**for**	her father.

When the indirect object is first, do not use *to* or *for*.

	Verb	To/For	Indirect Object	Direct Object
Alex	gave	~~to~~	Jane	flowers.
Laura	bought	~~for~~	her father	a car.

When the direct object is a pronoun (*me, you, him, her, it, us, them*), it normally comes first.

	Verb	Direct Object	To/For	Indirect Object
Alex	gave	**them**	to	Jane.
Laura	bought	**it**	for	her father.

A direct object answers the question *What?* An indirect object answers the questions *Who(m)* + *to* or *for*?

Questions	Answers
What did Alex give his wife?	He gave her **flowers**.
Who did Alex give flowers **to**?	He gave them **to his wife**.
Who did Laura buy a car **for**?	She bought a car **for her father**.

Not all verbs with indirect objects follow the same patterns. For example, look at the verb *explain*:

        Correct: John explained the problem to Mary.
        Incorrect: John explained Mary the problem.

1 Underline the direct object. Circle the indirect object.

Example:

Maria left <u>a letter</u> for (her daughter) on the dining room table.

  a. Maria's daughter, Eva, took the letter to a clerk at the bank.
  b. The clerk at the bank gave his boss the letter.
  c. The boss at the bank gave Eva some money.
  d. Eva brought the money to her mother.
  e. Maria bought a new refrigerator
     for her family.

2 Sara did a lot of things today. Look at the underlined words in the answers. Circle direct object (DO) or indirect object (IO). Then write the question.

Example:

Q: *What did Sara send?*
A: Sara sent <u>the letters</u>.   (DO)   IO
Q: *Who did Sara send the letters to?*
A: She sent the letters to <u>the customers</u>.   DO   (IO)

1. **Q:** _____?
   A: Sara sold her <u>computer</u>.   DO   IO

2. **Q:** _____?
   A: She sold her computer to <u>her neighbor</u>.   DO   IO

3. **Q:** _____?
   A: Sarah bought <u>some toys</u>.   DO   IO

4. **Q:** _____?
   A: She bought toys for <u>her nieces</u>.   DO   IO

5. **Q:** _____?
   A: She wrote a <u>report</u>.   DO   IO

6. **Q:** _____?
   A: She wrote a report to <u>her boss</u>.   DO   IO

3 Write **C** if the sentence is correct. Write **I** if the sentence is incorrect. Then correct the incorrect sentences.

a. _C_ Steve showed his girlfriend the letter. _____

b. _I_ He showed it her.   _He showed it to her._

c. ____ I always take her flowers.   _____

d. ____ We bought for you a present.   _____

e. ____ Angela told the children a story.   _____

f. ____ Would you mind giving to me a ride? _____

g. ____ Rachel bought candy her mother.   _____

h. ____ Please bring me that book.   _____

i. ____ Bill opened me the door.   _____

4 Read the conversation. Who or what is each object pronoun? Write the answers on page 48.

TONY: Hello, Jim. This is Tony. Can you give **(1.) me** a ride to school today?

JIM: Sure, I can give **(2.) you** a ride. No problem.

TONY: Great. Do you remember Joe and Al?

JIM: Yes, I remember **(3.) them**. Why?

TONY: They're having a party on Friday. Do you want to go?

JIM: Sure. I love parties. Who else is going to **(4.) it**?

TONY: My sister Anna is going. Do you know **(5.) her**?

JIM: No, but you showed **(6.) me** a picture of her.

TONY: Well, I'll introduce **(7.) you** to **(8.) her** tomorrow. You can invite your sister, too.

JIM: Great. Would you let **(9.) us** know Joe and Al's address?

TONY: Sure, I'll call you. Oh, and it's Al's birthday Friday, but we don't have to bring **(10.) him** presents.

1. me = _____Tony_____   6. me = _____
2. you = _____   7. you = _____
3. them = _____   8. her = _____
4. it = _____   9. us = _____
5. her = _____   10. him = _____

 5 **Express Yourself** Make a list of presents you would like to give your family members and friends, but don't write the people's names. Show your list of presents to a partner. Take turns asking and answering questions about who you are giving the presents to and why.

Example:

A: Who are you going to give the CD to?

B: I'm going to give the CD to my brother. He likes Mariah Carey.

LISTENING and SPEAKING

Listen: Party Plans

1 You are planning a party for a friend. What do you need to do? Who can you ask for help?

STRATEGY **2** **Before You Listen** Amanda Cantor is planning a party for the new library. She is going to ask some friends to help. Look at Amanda's notes in Exercise 3 below. What do you think she might ask them to do? Write three things.

3 Listen to Amanda's phone conversations. What is each person going to do? Complete Amanda's notes.

Janet:
• buy _____ and _____
• get bright _____
  at **Party! Party!** on _____
• buy _____ of each

Isabel:
• address _____
• put _____ on them
• need them on _____

Norman:
• pick up _____ from printer on
  _____
• take to _____
• at **A-1 Printing** on _____

Michael:
• pick up _____ from
  _____ on _____
• mail them on _____

Work in small groups. Check your answers. Ask and answer questions like these:

Who is buying the … ? Who is addressing the … ?

Pronunciation

  Listen and read. Then repeat the questions after the speaker.

> **Intonation with *Wh*– Questions**
>
> *Wh*– questions usually have falling intonation.
>
> What can I do?   Where is the party?
>
> Who is buying the food?   When do you need it?

 Listen to the questions. Then practice saying them to a partner. Use falling intonation.

   a. Where do you live?

   b. What's your phone number?

   c. Who is writing the invitations?

   d. Who is choosing the music?

   e. What kind of music do you want?

   f. Who is bringing the drinks?

Speak Out

Work in groups of four. Plan a party. Make a list of the things you have to do. Fill in the "Things to Do" column of the chart below.

Things to Do:	Name:

8 Now ask who is going to do each thing. Then fill in the person's name in the "Name" column of the chart on page 49.

Example:

> **A:** Who's going to choose the music?
>
> **B:** I'll choose the music. Who's going to buy the drinks?

STRATEGY **Refusing a Request** When you can't or don't want to do something for someone, you can refuse politely.

> I'm sorry, but I really don't have time to buy the food.
>
> I'd be happy to help you, but my car isn't working.

9 Join another group. Share your party plans. Tell who is doing what for your group's party. Which group is going to have the best party? Why?

READING and WRITING

Read About It

1 **Before You Read** Look at the brochure here and on the next page. Who do you think wrote it? Why?

Urban Homesteading: The Possible Dream

River City Department of Housing
City Hall
1 Center Street
River City, NY 13500

Before homesteading

What is urban homesteading?

Urban homesteading is a way for people **to own** a home in the city at a very low price but with a lot of work. First, urban homesteaders must find an old building in the city that no one lives in. Then they pay a small price to the government. After that, they have **to fix** the building to make it safe and **livable**, and they have to live in it. If they do all this, they own the building.

How does urban homesteading work?

Often, people homestead in groups. They choose an old apartment building and they fix an apartment for each family. They do a lot of the work together. Some people can fix walls, floors, and ceilings. Some people can build closets and cabinets. Some can put in kitchen sinks and bathrooms. Some can paint and clean up.

What are the problems?

- Homesteading is very hard work.
- Homesteading **requires** special **skills**. If homesteaders don't know how to fix a house, they have to learn.
- Homesteading takes a lot of time. Most people have jobs. They can work on their building only after work and on weekends.
- It usually takes years to finish the work and move in.
- Urban homesteading is not expensive, but it does require some money. Many homesteaders have very little money, and this makes their lives difficult.
- In a group homestead, people have to get along with each other and make decisions together.

Urban homesteader at work

Do homesteads ever fail?

Urban homesteading is a wonderful thing for many people, but it is not easy. Yes, some homesteaders **quit** and some homesteads **fail**.

However, most homesteaders **overcome** their problems. One day the work is finished and the people move into bright, clean, comfortable apartments. They have a beautiful home for very little money, and they have neighbors who are like family. For most urban homesteaders, it is **a dream come true**.

STRATEGY ▶ **Guessing the Meaning of a Word** Sometimes you can guess the meaning of a new word. As you read, you should:

- look for an explanation or definition of the new word in the sentence or paragraph.
- look at any pictures that show or explain something about the new word.
- look for other words in the sentence or paragraph that explain the meaning of the new word.

2 Find the words in bold type in the reading. Then use the context to match each word with its meaning.

____	**1.** urban	**a.**	to need
____	**2.** to own	**b.**	knowledge and ability
____	**3.** to fix	**c.**	to possess, not to rent
____	**4.** livable	**d.**	something wished for
____	**5.** to require	**e.**	to get past, not stop because of
____	**6.** skills	**f.**	to repair
____	**7.** to quit	**g.**	to stop, leave
____	**8.** to fail	**h.**	in the city
____	**9.** to overcome	**i.**	OK to live in
____	**10.** a dream come true	**j.**	to not work out, not succeed

3 Did you guess the meanings of any of the words in Exercise 2? What helped you guess? Compare your answers with a partner's.

4 Read the questions. Underline the answers in the brochure. Then check your answers with a partner.

a. Urban homesteaders have to do four things before they own their building. What are they?

b. Homesteaders need some special skills. What are they? Use *–ing* forms like "making."

c. What are some of the problems of homesteading? Name four.

d. What are some of the good things about homesteading? Name two.

Think About It

5 What do you like about homesteading? What don't you like?

6 If you could homestead in your city or town, would you do it? Why or why not?

Write About It

 7 **Before You Write** Mrs. Gibson wants her son Eric to do some errands for her. Eric found this note in the kitchen. Read the note.

> Eric,
>
> Would you please go to the supermarket and get some milk and coffee for Grandma? She's sick today and can't go out. Also, please pick up her medicine at the drugstore. Take everything to her apartment.
>
> Thanks,
>
> Mom

8 **Write** You want your brother, sister, or friend to do you a favor. Think of a real person and a real favor you might ask them to do. Write a note. Use Mrs. Gibson's note for a model. Be sure to give enough information.

9 **Check Your Writing** Reread your note. Answer the questions below. Then revise your note if necessary.

- Did you give enough information?
- Did you use direct and indirect objects correctly?
- Is your spelling correct?

GETTING STARTED

Warm Up

1 People can do many things in their lives. What do they usually do first? Next? Last? Number these events in order.

_____ buy a house _____ have grandchildren

_____ travel _____ retire from work

_____ get a job _____ learn another language

_____ be born _____ finish school

_____ get married _____ move to another city

_____ leave home _____ die

_____ have children _____ go to school

2 Work with a partner. Compare your answers. Discuss any differences you have.

I didn't know you lived in Greece.

  Listen and read.

THOMAS: Are these family photographs, Eleni?

ELENI: Yes, these are my Greek relatives. This is me when I was five, and these are my parents and grandparents.

THOMAS: That's you? Cute kid! And who are these people?

ELENI: My Aunt Sophie and Uncle Costas. Aunt Sophie is my father's sister, and Uncle Costas is his brother-in-law. And these are my cousins, Nicky and Alex.

THOMAS: So are your parents from Greece?

ELENI: My mother's American but my father's Greek. We lived in Greece when we took these pictures.

THOMAS: Really? I didn't know you lived in Greece. How long did you live there?

ELENI: Six years. I was born in Greece. My parents met when they were in college here, but after they finished school and got married, they lived in Greece.

THOMAS: But they came back again?

ELENI: Yes, and I grew up here. When I was six, my father got a job in New Jersey and we left Greece and moved here.

THOMAS: Can you speak Greek?

ELENI: I can't speak it, but I can understand it because my parents often spoke it at home. And of course, I could speak it when I was young. But after we came here, I learned English. Now I'm sorry I forgot my Greek. It would be great to speak it well.

THOMAS: Yeah, especially if you go there. Do you have relatives in Greece?

ELENI: Well, my grandparents are here. When my grandfather retired in 1995, he and my grandmother bought a house near us. Then after my mom died last year, they came to live with us. But I still have aunts and uncles and cousins in Greece. In fact, my cousin Alex is coming to visit us in August. He's my favorite cousin. He loves to travel.

THOMAS: Cool! I'd like to meet him.

ELENI: Oh, yeah. You'll like Alex. He's great.

 Answer these questions.

a. Is the family in the picture Eleni's mother's or her father's?

b. Where did Eleni's parents meet?

c. Where was Eleni born?

d. How old was Eleni when her family moved to the United States?

e. Could Eleni speak Greek when she was young?

f. Where do Eleni and her family live now?

g. Who does Eleni live with?

Building Vocabulary

5 **Vocabulary Check** Complete the paragraph with words from the box. Use each word only once.

returned	left
forgot	miss
grew up	was born
moved	find
got	understand

My grandfather **(1.)** _____ in Ireland in 1930. His parents **(2.)** _____ to New York in 1932, so he **(3.)** _____ in the United States. My great-grandmother **(4.)** _____ a job in a dress factory, but my great-grandfather couldn't **(5.)** _____ work in New York. He **(6.)** _____ his family and traveled around the country for several years looking for work. My grandfather was very young then, so he didn't **(7.)** _____ his father. He almost **(8.)** _____ him. When my great-grandfather **(9.)** _____ home, he was like a stranger. My great-grandfather couldn't **(10.)** _____ why his son wasn't happy to see him. It was difficult for both of them.

More Time Expressions

We use *in* with months and years.

Eleni was born **in** January.	Eleni's grandfather retired **in** 1995.

We use *on* with days and dates.

Thomas visited Eleni **on** Saturday.	Alex arrived **on** August 9th.

6 Complete the family record with information about you and your family. Use *in* or *on* where needed.

Family Record

My mother was born _____ (year).

My father was born _____ (year).

My _____ (brother/sister/cousin) was born _____ (month).

I was born _____ (date).

Talk About It

7 Work with a partner. Ask questions about your partner's family. Choose events from the list in Exercise 1 on page 53. Use *before you were born* or *after you were born*.

Example:

A: Did your parents travel before you were born?
B: Yes, and they also traveled after I was born.
A: Did your parents work after you were born?
B: My father did, but my mother stayed at home for a few months.

Asking Questions About the Past

Who

Question	Answer
Who lived in Greece?	**Eleni** lived in Greece.
Who did Eleni live with?	She lived with **her parents**.

What, When, Where

Question	Answer
What did Eleni show Thomas?	She showed him **pictures of her family**.
When did Eleni live in Greece?	She lived there **when she was young**. She lived there **from 1984 to 1990**.
Where did Eleni's parents move to?	They moved to **New Jersey**.

How long vs. How long ago

Question	Answer
How long did Eleni live in Greece?	She lived there **for seven years**.
How long ago did Eleni's parents move to New Jersey?	They moved there **twelve years ago**.

 It's now 9:00 p.m. on October 26, 2000.
How long ago did Sue do the things in the list?
Work with a partner.

   a. had dinner at twenty after eight
   b. took a shower at seven o'clock
   c. got a new job on October 25th
   d. moved to a new house on October 12th
   e. got married on September 26th
   f. went to Buenos Aires on vacation in October, 1998

Example:

A: How long ago did she have dinner?
B: She had dinner forty minutes ago.

2 This time line shows John's life from 1989 to 1999. Work with a
partner. Ask and answer information questions about John.

1989	1990	1991	1992	1993	1994	1995	1996	1997	1998	1999

went to college

lived in New Jersey

worked in a bank

traveled in Asia

lived in Tokyo

Example:

A: How long did John go to college?
B: He went to college for four years.
B: When did he go to college?
A: He went to college from 1989 to 1993.

3 Look at the underlined words in the sentences. Then write the correct
questions. Use your own paper.

Example:

<u>Lucy</u> went out to dinner. = *Who went out to dinner?*

a. She went <u>to Gino's Italian Restaurant</u>.
b. She went with <u>her cousin and her aunt</u>.
c. They arrived at the restaurant <u>at eight o'clock</u>.
d. They stayed there <u>for three hours</u>.
e. They talked about <u>their family</u>.
f. She had <u>pasta and salad</u> for dinner.
g. They left the restaurant <u>an hour ago</u>.
h. Lucy got home <u>at 11:30</u>.
i. <u>Her cousin</u> drove her home.
j. She went to bed <u>at midnight</u>.

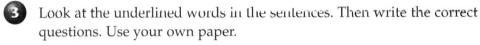

Asking About Past Ability

We use *could* and *couldn't* to talk about ability in the past.

Question	Short Answer
Could Eleni **speak** Greek twelve years ago?	Yes, she **could**.
Could she **speak** English when she was very young?	No, she **couldn't**.

4 What can you do now? Could you do those things five years ago? Add two more activities to the chart. Check (✓) *can*, *can't*, *could*, or *couldn't*.

		Now		Five Years Ago	
		can	*can't*	*could*	*couldn't*
a.	swim	☐	☐	☐	☐
b.	use e-mail	☐	☐	☐	☐
c.	speak English	☐	☐	☐	☐
d.	rollerblade	☐	☐	☐	☐
e.	cook	☐	☐	☐	☐
f.	_____	☐	☐	☐	☐
g.	_____	☐	☐	☐	☐

5 Work with a partner. What can your partner do? What could he or she do five years ago?

Example:

A: Can you swim?
B: Yes, I can.
A: Could you swim five years ago?
B: No, I couldn't. I learned to swim two years ago.

 6 **Express Yourself** Work with a partner. Find out about your partner's childhood.

Example:

A: Where did you grow up?   A: How long did you live there?
B: I grew up in Boca Raton, Florida.   B: I lived there for ten years.

LISTENING and SPEAKING

Listen: A Family Conversation

1 What do you do when you visit your relatives? What do you talk about?

② **Before You Listen** You can understand a conversation better if you already know something about the speakers and the situation. Eleni is meeting Alex at the airport. Look at the conversation on page 54. Answer these questions:

    a. Where does Eleni live?   **d.** Who is Alex's father?

    b. Who is Alex?   **e.** Who is Nicky?

    c. Where does Alex live?

③ Read the two lists below. Listen to the conversation and write the name of the correct person at the top of each list.

Person 1: _____	Person 2: _____
____ finished school	____ retired
____ traveled a lot	____ started acting
____ got a job in Piraeus	____ met a woman
____ moved to Athens	____ wife got sick
____ bought a house	____ wife died
____ got married	____ sat around the house

④ Listen again. Number the events in each list in Exercise 3 from 1 (first) to 6 (last). Write the numbers in the spaces.

Pronunciation

the –ed ending

We pronounce the –ed ending of past tense verbs in three ways. The pronunciation depends on the final sound of the verb.

/d/	/t/	/ɪd/
liste**n** + ed	hel**p** + ed	wan**t** + ed ad**d** + ed

⑤ Listen to the words. Check (✓) the sound you hear.

	/d/	/t/	/ɪd/			/d/	/t/	/ɪd/
a. laughed	☐	☐	☐		**e.** painted	☐	☐	☐
b. called	☐	☐	☐		**f.** helped	☐	☐	☐
c. needed	☐	☐	☐		**g.** loved	☐	☐	☐
d. learned	☐	☐	☐		**h.** invited	☐	☐	☐

Speak Out

⑥ Work with a partner. Tell each other something about your past. Then ask and answer at least three questions to get more details. Make notes to remember your partner's answers.

Example:

A: We moved when I was ten.

B: Where did you move to?

A: We moved to a farm.

B: How long did you live there?

A: We lived there for thirteen years.

 STRATEGY **Checking Information** If you aren't sure what a person said, you can ask for clarification.

> B: Did you say *thirteen* or *thirty*?
>
> A: Thir*teen*.

 Work in groups of four. Tell the group about your partner from Exercise 6.

READING and WRITING

Read About It

 Before You Read Look at the photograph. Where are the people? Are they working or playing? Is it safe or dangerous?

The Great Wallendas: At Home in the Air

Karl Wallenda was born in Germany in 1905 and grew up in a big circus family. He began performing when he was six years old. Many of
5 Karl's relatives were in the circus— his parents, his brother Herman, his aunt, and his grandparents. The family tradition goes back to 1780, when the Wallendas were circus
10 performers in Europe.

In 1925, in Milan, Italy, the Wallendas performed a four-person pyramid for the first time. John Ringling, from the Ringling Brothers
15 and Barnum & Bailey Circus, saw the

The Great Wallendas performing the seven-person pyramid

act and invited the Wallendas to move to the United States and work for his circus. The Great Wallendas worked for "The Greatest Show on Earth" for seventeen years and performed for hundreds of audiences.

A turning point for the Great Wallendas came in 1947,
20 a year after they left Ringling Brothers. Karl introduced a new
act: the seven-person pyramid. Before the Great Wallendas,
people thought the seven-person pyramid was impossible, but
the Wallendas performed it safely for many years. Then, in
1962, there was an accident. Four of the seven people fell to
25 the ground. Three of them died and one, Karl's son, was
paralyzed and could not walk again.

The Wallendas continued to perform, but they did not
perform the seven-person pyramid. Karl Wallenda died in
1978 when he fell from a high wire in San Juan, Puerto Rico.
30 He was 73 years old.

Today, however, Karl's grandchildren and great-
grandchildren are performing the seven-person pyramid again. They re-created it for
the first time in 1998, in the same building where the 1962 accident happened. Karl
Wallenda once said, "Life is being on the wire. Everything else is just waiting." The
35 young Wallendas are continuing this circus family's great tradition.

STRATEGY **Scanning for Important Information** Sometimes dates and numbers can give you important information quickly.

 Read these questions. Then look for dates and numbers in the
reading. Underline the answers to the questions.

  a. How long ago were the Wallendas a circus family?

  b. How long did the Wallendas work for the Ringling Brothers and
Barnum & Bailey Circus?

  c. When did the Wallendas leave the Ringling Brothers and Barnum
& Bailey Circus?

  d. When did they start performing the seven-person pyramid?

  e. What happened in 1962?

  f. When did Karl Wallenda die? What happened?

  g. How long was he a performer?

  h. Who re-created the seven-person pyramid in 1998?

 Vocabulary Check Match the words with their meanings.
Write the letters on the lines.

_____ **1.** tradition (line 8)	**a.**	not able to move
_____ **2.** to perform (line 12)	**b.**	to do again
_____ **3.** act (line 16)	**c.**	history
_____ **4.** audience (line 18)	**d.**	people watching a performance
_____ **5.** accident (line 24)	**e.**	to do something for people to watch
_____ **6.** paralyzed (line 26)	**f.**	something unplanned; usually bad
_____ **7.** to re-create (line 32)	**g.**	the four-person pyramid; the seven-person pyramid

Think About It

 Read the statements. Do you agree or disagree? Why?
- Karl Wallenda liked doing dangerous things.
- The Wallenda family has a great tradition.

5 Would you like to perform for audiences? What kind of act would you like to do?

Write About It

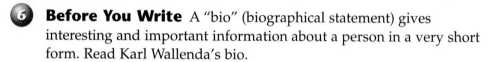

STRATEGY **6** **Before You Write** A "bio" (biographical statement) gives interesting and important information about a person in a very short form. Read Karl Wallenda's bio.

Karl Wallenda

1905	Born into a circus family in Germany
1925	Created and performed the first four-person high-wire pyramid
1927	Married Martha Schepp
1928	Traveled to the United States to work with the Ringling Brothers and Barnum & Bailey Circus
1930	Got divorced from Martha Schepp
1935	Married Helen Kreis
1946	Left Ringling Brothers' circus
1947	Performed the seven-person pyramid for the first time
1978	Fell during a high-wire act and died at age 73

---

7 **Write** Write twelve things that happened to you or things that you did in the past. Write the dates. Choose six or seven important things from your list. On a separate piece of paper, write them in order from first to last. Use Karl Wallenda's bio as a model.

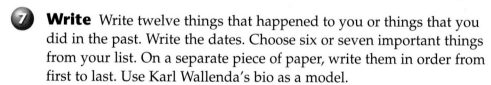 **8** **Check Your Writing** Use the questions to check your bio. Revise your bio if necessary.

- Are your points important and interesting?
- Are they in the correct order?
- Did you use the past tense correctly?

1 Complete the conversations with the correct form of *have to, can,* or *could.*

    PIA: (1.) _____ you help me this afternoon?

    JOE: I'm sorry but I (2.) _____. I (3.) _____ go shopping with my mother.

    ANN: (4.) _____ you drive when you were sixteen?

    DAN: Yes, I (5.) _____. My grandfather gave me an old car and I (6.) _____ learn to drive it.

    ANN: Was it hard?

    DAN: Driving was easy, but parking was hard. I (7.) _____ park well at first.

    CARLOS: Do you ever work on Sundays?

    JUAN: Yes, I do. I (8.) _____ work on Sundays, but sometimes I want to. I need the money.

2 Complete the sentences. Put the words and phrases in parentheses in the correct order.

  a. Beto **(me/a job/got)** _____.

  b. My grandmother **(gave/me/to/this)** _____.

  c. Somebody **(you/this message/left/for)** _____.

  d. Who **(sent/me/these photographs)** _____?

  e. Elinor **(the airport/to/her boss/took)** _____.

3 On a separate piece of paper rewrite each pair of sentences as one sentence. Do not change the order of the sentences. Use *before, after,* or *when.*

Example:

Laura finished school. She needed to get a job.

When Laura finished school, she needed to get a job.

  a. Laura talked to a career counselor. She didn't know what kind of job she wanted.

  b. The counselor asked Laura questions. She had to think about her likes and dislikes.

  c. The counselor asked Laura to take a test. She answered all his questions.

  d. Laura took the test. The counselor read it.

  e. The counselor explained the test results to Laura. They met again.

  f. The counselor gave Laura good ideas. She started looking for a job.

4 Read the bio of Eleni's friend Thomas. Write information questions to complete Alex and Eleni's conversation about Thomas. Use the question words in the box. Use each question word once.

> How
> How long
> How long ago
> When
> Where
> Who

Thomas Mercer

1982 Born in California

1984 Parents died
Went to live with his aunt and uncle

1992 Moved to Jersey City to live with his grandparents

1995 Started high school

1997 Moved to Hoboken

1998 Started at Eleni's high school in the fall

1999 Met Eleni in chemistry class

ALEX: (1.) _____?
ELENI: In California. His parents died when he was very young.
ALEX: That's too bad. (2.) _____?
ELENI: With his aunt and uncle, I think. He lives with his grandparents now.
ALEX: (3.) _____?
ELENI: In 1992.
ALEX: (4.) _____?
ELENI: For about five years. He started high school there.
ALEX: (5.) _____?
ELENI: Three years ago.
ALEX: (6.) _____?
ELENI: I met him in my chemistry class.

Vocabulary Review

Complete the paragraph below. Use the correct forms of the verbs in the box. You will use some of the words more than once.

> be   get   miss
> do   have   move
> finish make   retire

After Maggie Benning **(1.)** _____ college, she **(2.)** _____ a job as a librarian in a small town in Vermont. She didn't **(3.)** _____ much money, but she enjoyed her work. She fell in love and **(4.)** _____ married when she was twenty-six. The next year, she **(5.)** _____ a baby. Maggie and her husband **(6.)** _____ their best, but they **(7. neg.)** _____ happy. They **(8.)** _____ a divorce, and Maggie **(9.)** _____ a decision. She **(10.)** _____ from her job and **(11.)** _____ to Mexico. She **(12.)** _____ her friends, but she's very happy in her new life.

ARE YOU HUNGRY?

Menu

Soups	cup	bowl
Tomato	1.75	2.75
Onion	2.00	3.00
Vegetable	2.50	4.00
Chicken	2.50	4.00

Salads

Green salad	2.75
(lettuce, tomatoes, onions)	
Three-bean salad	2.25
(white, red, and green beans)	
Potato salad	2.25
(potatoes, onions, carrots)	

Sandwiches

(Served on whole wheat or white bread)

Chicken salad	4.50
Egg salad	3.25
Grilled cheese	3.00

Pizza & Pasta	small	large
Cheese pizza	6.95	9.95
Slice of pizza	1.75	
Spaghetti with meat sauce	4.95	
Spaghetti with garlic and olive oil	4.25	

Main Dishes

(Served with bread and butter and two side dishes)

Fried chicken	5.95
Stir-fried beef	6.95
Broiled fish	6.50
Broiled hamburger *(100% beef)*	5.25

Vegetarian Dishes

(Served with bread and butter; hot dishes served with two side dishes)

Steamed vegetables	4.95
Vegetable omelet	4.95
(eggs with cheese and vegetables, served with fried potatoes)	
Black beans and rice	3.75
Fruit and cheese plate	6.50

Side Dishes

French fries	1.25
Mashed potatoes	1.00
Rice *(brown or white)*	1.00
Green beans	1.75
Carrots	1.75
Applesauce	1.25

Desserts

Cheesecake	2.95
Chocolate cake	2.35
Apple pie *(served hot or cold)*	2.75
Brownie	1.00
Ice cream *(chocolate or vanilla)*	2.00

Drinks	small	large
Juice	.75	1.25
(orange, apple, tomato)		
Milk		1.25
Soft drinks	.85	1.25
Coffee or Tea		1.35

GETTING STARTED

Warm Up

1 Work with a partner. Ask and answer the questions about the menu.

a. I want eggs. What can I order? What else can I order?

b. I don't eat meat or fish. What part of the menu is for me?

c. I'm a vegetarian. Can I order spaghetti?

d. I like beef, but I don't like fried food. What can I eat?

e. I only have $5.00. Can I buy a cup of soup and a sandwich?

f. I want fried chicken with apple sauce, green beans, and carrots. How much will I pay?

g. I want chocolate cake and a small glass of milk for dessert. Can I have that?

h. What would you order from the menu?

What's for dinner?

A.

MRS. LEE: The soup smells delicious, Steve. How do you make it?

STEVE: The recipe is easy, Mom. First, I cut up a few onions and fry them with a little beef. Then I add some water. Next, I cut up some potatoes and carrots and add them to the soup. And I add a can of beans. After that, I add a can of tomato juice and some salt and pepper. I stir everything together and cook it for an hour. Do you want to taste it?

MRS. LEE: Sure. Mmmm. It tastes great! I can't believe you're learning to cook.

STEVE: I *have* to cook. College is expensive, and I can't eat in restaurants all the time. Do we need anything else for dinner?

MRS. LEE: Well, we need some dessert. How much fruit is there in the refrigerator?

STEVE: There's a lot of fruit. There's a bunch of grapes, two bananas, and a few oranges.

MRS. LEE: How about making a fruit salad? Oh, and is there any bread?

STEVE: I don't see any. And there's only a little milk. I'll go to the store and get some bread and milk before I make the fruit salad.

MRS. LEE: OK. And get a pound of butter, too. It's nice to have you home. I missed you.

STEVE: I missed you too, Mom. It's nice to be home for a few days.

B.

LISA: Hi! What's for dinner?

MRS. LEE: Hi, Lisa. Steve made soup. Would you set the table, please? The knives, forks, and spoons are in the dishwasher. The clean glasses are on the counter. The napkins are in the cupboard.

LISA: OK. Mom, is this right?

MRS. LEE: Yes, that's right. The napkins and forks go on the left. The knives and spoons go on the right. But tonight we don't need forks—there's just soup and fruit salad.

3 Answer these questions.

    a. What kind of soup is Steve making?

    b. How long does Steve have to cook the soup?

    c. What is Steve going to buy at the store?

    d. What is Steve going to make for dessert?

    e. Does Steve live at home now? How do you know?

    f. How do you set the table? Draw a picture with a partner.

Building Vocabulary

4 **Vocabulary Check** Match the underlined word or words in each sentence with a word from the list. Write the letters on the lines.

_____	**1.** Before I cook, I read the <u>directions</u>.	**a.** add
_____	**2.** I <u>cook</u> a few carrots and onions <u>in hot oil</u>.	**b.** cup
_____	**3.** Then I <u>put in</u> the pieces of chicken.	**c.** delicious
_____	**4.** I put in some salt and <u>mix</u> it in.	**d.** dessert
_____	**5.** Then I <u>put the food on the plates</u>.	**e.** fry
_____	**6.** The stir fried chicken always tastes <u>very good</u>.	**f.** recipe
_____	**7.** I usually drink a <u>small container</u> of tea after dinner.	**g.** stir
_____	**8.** After the main dish, I eat <u>something sweet</u>.	**h.** serve

Adjectives Ending with –ed

The –ed form of a verb (past participle) is sometimes used as an adjective.

> We had **grilled** cheese sandwiches for lunch.
>
> I made **fried** chicken for dinner last night.

5 Look at the menu on page 65. Underline five more –ed adjectives. What food does each adjective describe?

Adjectives Following Linking Verbs:
Sound, Look, Feel, Taste, Smell, Be

These verbs are usually followed by an adjective. The adjective describes the subject.

That music **sounds** great.	The sun **feels** hot.	This food **tastes** delicious.
His shirt **looks** dirty.	The milk **smells** terrible.	The soup **is** excellent.

6 Write a sentence on a separate piece of paper with each word in the list. Use *sound, look, feel, taste,* or *smell.* Then work with a partner and compare your sentences.

Example:

Her voice sounds beautiful.

a. beautiful	**c.** clean	**e.** dangerous	**g.** fresh	**i.** expensive
b. good	**d.** cold	**f.** delicious	**h.** easy	**j.** terrible

Talk About It

7 Work in groups. You are going to have lunch together three days next week. Plan a different menu for each day. Choose food that everyone likes. Use the menu on page 65 or your own ideas.

Monday	Wednesday	Friday

GRAMMAR

Count/Non-count Nouns

Count nouns are nouns we can count. They have a plural form. We use *a* or *an* before singular count nouns.

> I ate **an orange** and **two muffins** this morning.
>
> We need **an egg**, **a tomato**, and **an onion**.
>
> I bought **oranges**, **eggs**, **onions**, and **tomatoes**.

Non-count nouns are nouns we do not usually count. They do not have a plural form. We do not usually use *a* or *an* before a non-count noun.

> Steve never drinks **milk**.
>
> When I'm sick, I like **cereal** and **tea**.
>
> We eat **rice** every day.

1 Complete the chart. Write *a/an* for count nouns. Write ✗ for non-count nouns. Write the plural form if there is one.

Singular		Plural	Singular		Plural
a.	✗ coffee	✗	g.	___ potato	_____
b.	a dish	dishes	h.	___ egg	_____
c.	___ dollar	_____	i.	___ spoon	_____
d.	___ hot dog	_____	j.	___ soup	_____
e.	___ ice cream	_____	k.	___ sugar	_____
f.	___ money	_____	l.	___ water	_____

Talking About Non-specific Quantities

We use certain expressions to talk about non-specific quantities of count and non-count nouns.

Count Nouns

How many onions does Steve need?

He needs **a few** onions.

He also needs **some** carrots.

He needs **a lot of** potatoes, but he doesn't need **many** beans.

He doesn't need **any** eggs.

Non-count Nouns

How much milk does Mrs. Lee have?

Mrs. Lee has a **little** milk.

She needs **some** bread.

She needs **a lot of** butter, but she doesn't need **much** rice.

She doesn't need **any** fruit.

---

2 Complete the conversation. Use *a few, a little, much, many,* or *any.*

SUE: How (1.) _____ bread do we have?

BOB: We don't have (2.) _____ bread. I ate the last piece.

SUE: Well, we need some for dinner. How (3.) _____ milk is there?

BOB: There's only (4.) _____ milk. I'll go to the store. Do we need anything else?

SUE: Well, there's enough chicken and rice, but we need (5.) _____ carrots.

BOB: How (6.) _____ carrots do you want?

SUE: Get a pound. Oh, and would you buy some fruit, too?

BOB: Sure. I'll get (7.) _____ apples and pears.

Talking About Specific Quantities

To talk about a specific quantity of a count or non-count noun, we can use units of measure or containers.

Count	Non-count	Count or Non-count
a **bunch of** grapes	a **liter of** gas	a **pound of** tomatoes, butter
a **package of** nuts	a **quart of** juice	a **kilo of** grapes, cheese
a **bag of** potato chips	a **cup of** coffee	a **bowl of** cherries, soup
	a **glass of** water	a **serving of** potatoes, fruit
		a **can of** beans, tuna
		a **carton of** eggs, milk

3 Complete the conversation. Choose the correct expression from the box and write it in the space. More than one answer may be correct.

a bag of	a bunch of	a can of	a package of	a bottle of
a pound of	a carton of	a quart of	a loaf of	a box of

HEIDI: Hi, Grandma. This is Heidi. I'm going to the store. Can I get you anything?

GRANDMA: Oh, yes, dear. I need several things. I need **(1.)** _____ tuna fish, **(2.)** _____ sugar, and **(3.)** _____ coffee.

HEIDI: Wait a minute! I'm writing this down … OK.

GRANDMA: **(4.)** _____ orange juice, **(5.)** _____ grapes, **(6.)** _____ milk.

HEIDI: What else?

GRANDMA: Now, let me think. Oh, I need **(7.)** _____ water and **(8.)** _____ whole wheat bread. And **(9.)** _____ butter. That's all. And get yourself **(10.)** _____ cookies.

HEIDI: OK, Grandma. See you soon. Bye!

 4 **Express Yourself**

a. Make a shopping list for the supermarket. Write ten kinds of food.

b. Work with a partner. You are going to go to the supermarket for your partner. Ask your partner questions so that you can buy *exactly* what he or she wants. Ask how much? How many? What kind? Make notes on the list.

Listen: Making Chicken Cacciatore

1 Can you cook? Do you use a recipe when you cook? What kinds of information are in a recipe?

STRATEGY **2** **Before You Listen** Read the incomplete recipe for chicken cacciatore in Exercise 3 below. Is it a main dish or a side dish? What is in it? Does it sound good to you?

 3 Listen to the recipe and write the missing words.

You need garlic, **(1.)** _____ pounds of chicken, **(2.)** _____ onions, and four **(3.)** _____ of tomatoes.

(4.) _____ the chicken into pieces. **(5.)** _____ the pieces in hot **(6.)** _____. Slice the onions and **(7.)** _____ them. **(8.)** _____ the garlic and fry it, too. Add the chicken and the **(9.)** _____ and some salt and pepper and cook for **(10.)** _____ minutes. Then put the cacciatore in the oven and bake it for **(11.)** _____ hours. **(12.)** _____ it with rice.

Pronunciation

Intonation: Words in a List

Use rising intonation before the commas in a list of words. Use falling intonation after the word *and*.

A green salad is lettuce, tomatoes, *and* onions.

Three-bean salad has white, red, *and* green beans.

4 Listen to these sentences. Then practice them with a partner. Check your intonation.

   a. We have coffee, tea, and milk.
   b. It comes with soup, a salad, and dessert.
   c. There are oranges, grapes, apples, and bananas.
   d. We have cheesecake, chocolate cake, apple pie, and brownies.

Speak Out

STRATEGY **Asking Someone to Speak Slowly** When you are listening and writing at the same time, you can say:

Go slowly, please. I'm writing this down.   Can you please say that again?

5 Work with a partner. You and your partner are
going to make dinner for some friends.
You are talking on the phone.
You need these things.

4 chickens	a lot of garlic
2 pounds of rice	5 bananas
4 oranges	1 can of coffee
7 tomatoes	2 cartons of apple juice
1 pound of grapes	

One of you has the things on Table A on this page. The other has the things on
Table B on page 74. Talk about the things you have and need. Each of you should
make a shopping list. Then compare your lists. Are they the same?

Example:

A: We need four oranges. How many oranges do you have?

B: I have one.

A: I have two. We need to buy one orange.

READING and WRITING

Read About It

1 **Before You Read** Think about the food you ate yesterday. What
food do you think was good for you? What food wasn't?

STRATEGY **Using Pictures** Before you start to read, always look at any pictures that
go with the text. These will help you understand the reading.

2 Look at the picture of the food pyramid.
What foods can you name?

1. _____

2. _____

3. _____

4. _____

5. _____

6. _____

The Food Pyramid*

Bread, Cereal, Rice, and Pasta: 6–11 servings a day

1 serving = 1 slice of bread; 1/2 cup of rice or pasta

These foods have a lot of carbohydrates. Choose whole-grain products like whole-wheat bread and brown rice for lots of fiber, vitamins, and minerals.

Fruit: 2–4 servings a day

1 serving = 1 medium apple, banana, or orange; 1/2 cup of chopped fruit; 3/4 cup of fruit juice

Fruit has a lot of vitamins, not much fat, and not many calories. Choose fresh fruit and fruit juice. Don't choose processed fruit with added sugar, like canned fruit salad.

Vegetables: 3–5 servings a day

1 serving = 1 cup of chopped lettuce; 1/2 cup of other chopped vegetables; 3/4 cup of vegetable juice

Vegetables have vitamins and fiber, and little or no fat. You need dark green vegetables, yellow or orange vegetables, and starchy vegetables like potatoes.

Meat, Poultry, Fish, Beans, Eggs, and Nuts: 2–3 servings a day

1 serving = a small piece (the size of an egg) of cooked meat, poultry, or fish; 1 egg; 1/2 cup of cooked beans; a handful of seeds or nuts

Meat, poultry, fish, and eggs have the most protein. Choose meat without much fat. Beans, nuts, and seeds also have protein. They also have a lot of fiber and some vitamins and minerals.

Milk, Yogurt, and Cheese: 2–3 servings a day

1 serving = 1 cup of milk or yogurt, a small piece of cheese

Milk products have the most calcium (an important mineral). They also have protein and some vitamins. Choose milk products with no fat or a little fat.

Fats, Oils, and Sweets: Use very little.

These foods have a lot calories, and they don't have other things you need in food. Choose olive oil instead of butter.

*Adapted from *United States Department of Agriculture 1995 Dietary Guidelines*

 3 Complete the food pyramid on page 72. Write the names of the food groups on the lines.

4 Why is there an asterisk (*) after the title, "The Food Pyramid?"

Think About It

5 Do you eat too much of some foods? Which ones?

6 Do you need to eat more of some foods? Which ones?

Write About It

 7 **Before You Write** People write journals to remember things. They write about what they do and what they think. Make a list of everything you ate yesterday. Write everything you can remember. When you are ready, organize your list. What did you eat in each food group?

Now read this journal paragraph about food.

> Yesterday, I didn't eat very well. I ate too much bread and rice, and I didn't choose whole grains I ate a banana and I drank some orange juice, but I didn't eat enough fruit. I didn't eat any green or yellow vegetables. I had some little tomatoes and they were delicious. But I need to eat more vegetables. I had a lot of beans for lunch, with rice. I think I had three servings. I always drink a lot of milk and I had three glasses of milk yesterday—about four servings. I ate too much fat and sugar. I had a lot of butter on my bread, and I ate two pieces of pie with ice cream. It's the same every day. I want to eat well, but I don't enjoy food that is good for me.

8 **Write** Write a journal paragraph about what you ate yesterday. Answer these questions. Did you eat well or not? For each food group, did you eat enough? Too much? How do you feel about this?

 9 **Check Your Writing** Use the editing checklist below. Revise your journal entry as necessary.

- Did you mention every food group?
- Did you write about quantities correctly?
- Did you use the past tense correctly?

GETTING STARTED

Warm Up

1 Look at the accidents in pictures 1–4. Who do you call in case of each accident? Write the letter of the picture in the correct box.

What happened?

2 Listen and read.

BEN: Mike! It's Ben. What happened? Did you forget about lunch?

MIKE: No, I didn't forget. I'm really sorry I didn't get there, but it wasn't my fault. Let me tell you what happened.

BEN: OK. I'm listening.

MIKE: Well, while I was walking to the bus stop, I saw an accident. A woman was crossing the street when she tripped and fell in front of traffic.

BEN: Was she all right?

MIKE: Well, she hurt her arm, but she was lucky. A truck was coming right at her and it almost hit her, but the driver stopped in time.

BEN: Wow! But why did that make you late?

MIKE: Well, the woman was really upset, so I stayed with her until the ambulance came.

BEN: Why didn't you call me?

MIKE: I *did* call you. I called your cell phone, but you didn't answer.

BEN: Oh, right. I left it at home this morning.

MIKE: And I couldn't call the restaurant because I couldn't remember the name. I only had the address.

BEN: OK, OK. But you never came. What else happened?

MIKE: Well, I missed my bus. Then, while I was waiting for the next bus, I went into a store, and while I was looking around, I smelled smoke.

BEN: Oh, no.

MIKE: Oh, yes. People were shouting, "Fire!" Everyone was running out of the store, so I started to run, too. I wasn't looking down, so I tripped and fell and hurt my knee.

BEN: Is it OK?

MIKE: Yeah, but I had to go to the emergency room to check it.

BEN: Oh, bad luck!

MIKE: I know. I called you when I got home, but there was no answer.

BEN: Yeah, I was probably still at the restaurant. Actually, I met a woman while I was waiting for you.

MIKE: You did?

BEN: Yeah. Her name's Arlene and she's really cool.

MIKE: I can't believe it! While I was in the emergency room, you were meeting a woman! Some people have all the luck.

3 Match the two parts of the sentences. Write the letters on the lines.

_____ **1.** Mike was walking to the bus stop when

_____ **2.** The woman was upset, so

_____ **3.** Mike went into a store while

_____ **4.** While Mike was looking around,

_____ **5.** Mike went to the emergency room because

_____ **6.** Ben didn't answer his cell phone because

_____ **7.** Ben met a woman while

a. he was waiting for the next bus.

b. he smelled smoke.

c. Mike stayed with her.

d. it was at home.

e. a woman fell in the street.

f. he was waiting for Mike.

g. he hurt his knee.

Building Vocabulary

 4 **Vocabulary Check** Complete the paragraph with words from the box. Use the correct form.

fall	forget	remember	hit	lucky	until
fault	miss	shout	hurt	still	upset

I saw an accident yesterday on First Street. A man started to cross the street when the light was red. A woman on a motorcycle
(1.) _____ him and he **(2.)** _____ down. The woman jumped off her motorcycle and ran to him. She looked very
(3.) _____. The man said, "Don't worry. You didn't
(4.) _____ me." Then the woman got mad. She
(5.) _____, "You're really **(6.)** _____, you know! The light was red!" The man said, "I know. It wasn't your
(7.) _____. I **(8.)** _____ to look. Sorry." The man was **(9.)** _____ sitting in the street. The woman helped him up and then she waited **(10.)** _____ he walked away. Next time he'll probably **(11.)** _____ to look before crossing the street.

Expressions with *Time*

There are many common expressions with the word *time*.

> Rick is always late. He never comes **on time**.
>
> I turned off the stove before the eggs burned. I turned it off **in time**.
>
> I was very busy all day today, so I didn't **have time** to make dinner.
>
> Lois had fun at the club last night. She always **has a good time** when she dances with her friends.
>
> If you don't finish your work before closing time, you will have to work **overtime**.

5 Complete each sentence with one of the expressions above. Use each expression only once.

Tom: Maria's party will be a lot of fun. I'm sure we'll **(1.)** _____.

Sandy: Don't be late. Maria wants everyone to come **(2.)** _____.

Tom: Well, I won't be there when it starts, but I'll arrive **(3.)** _____ to have cake.

Sandy: Is your sister going to the party, too?

Tom: No, she doesn't **(4.)** _____. She's working **(5.)** _____ at the restaurant.

Talk About It

 Work with a partner. Follow these steps:
- Think about an accident or an emergency that you remember.
- Get ready to describe it in five or six sentences.
- Tell your partner your story. Listen to your partner's story.
- Work with a new partner. Tell your first partner's story.

GRAMMAR

The Past Progressive Tense: Statements

We use the past progressive tense (*was/were* + verb *–ing*) to talk about an action that was in progress (*was happening*) at a specific time in the past.

> The police officer worked from 9:00 a.m. until 5:00 p.m. yesterday.
> She **was working** at 1:30 p.m.   She **was not working** at 5:30 p.m.
>
> The firefighters worked from 10:00 p.m. until 4:00 a.m. yesterday.
> They **were working** at midnight.   They **were not working** at 6:00 a.m.

 was + not = wasn't
were + not = weren't

 Write sentences about the Nelson family. Use the words below and any other words you need. Use the past progressive tense.

Example:

Sue Nelson/visit a friend/four o'clock

Sue Nelson was visiting a friend at four o'clock.

a. Greg Nelson and his friend/play tennis/three-thirty

_____

b. the Nelson's three cats/sleep under the couch/four-thirty

_____

c. the Nelson's neighbors/eat dinner/five o'clock

_____

d. Mrs. Nelson/work in her office/five-thirty

_____

e. Mr. Nelson/drive home from the office/six o'clock

_____

f. the Nelson's dog/play with a ball/six-thirty

_____

The Past Progressive: Questions

Yes/No Questions	Short Answers
Was the police officer **working** at 4:00 p.m.?	Yes, she **was**.
Were the firefighters **working** at 9:00 p.m.?	No, they **weren't**.
Information Questions	**Answers**
Where **was** the police officer **working**?	She **was working** downtown.
What **were** the firefighters **doing**?	They **were fighting** a fire.

 2 Work with a partner. Look at Exercise 1 on page 78. Ask and answer questions about the Nelson family.

Example:

A: What was Sue Nelson doing at four o'clock?

B: She was visiting a friend.

When and *While* Clauses

When and *while* clauses show that two actions happened at the same time. Use *when* to show a finished action. Use *while* to show an action in progress.

> Sue was washing the dishes **when Luis called**.
>
> **When Luis called**, Sue was washing the dishes.
>
> Sue broke a plate **while** they **were talking**.
>
> **While** they **were talking**, Sue broke a plate.

 Both actions can be in progress at the same time:
While they **were talking** on the phone, Luis **was making** dinner.

3 Circle the correct answers.

    a. The verb after *when* is in the (simple past, past progressive)

    b. The verb after *while* is in the (simple past, past progressive)

    c. If the sentence begins with *when* or *while*, (use, don't use) a comma after the first clause.

4 Complete the sentences with *when* or *while*.

    a. Mrs. Nelson was talking on the telephone _____ she heard a noise.

    b. Greg heard the noise _____ he was cleaning his room.

    c. Sue was studying _____ she heard the noise.

    d. _____ Mr. Nelson heard the noise, he was reading the newspaper.

    e. The cats broke a lamp _____ they were playing.

    f. The dog was sleeping _____ the cats were playing.

    g. The dog woke up _____ she heard the noise.

    h. In the next apartment, the neighbors were watching TV _____ the lamp broke. They didn't hear the noise.

Because and So Clauses

Because clauses give reasons.

> Why did Mike have to go to the emergency room?
>
> He went to the emergency room **because he hurt his foot**.
>
> Why didn't Ben answer his cell phone?
>
> He didn't answer it **because it was at home**.

So clauses give results.

> Mike hurt his foot, **so he went to the emergency room**.
>
> Ben left his cell phone at home, **so he couldn't answer it**.

5 Check (✓) the correct answer.

   a. The action in a *because* clause happens   ☐ first   ☐ second.

   b. The action in a *so* clause happens   ☐ first   ☐ second.

6 Circle *because* or *so* to complete these sentences. Add a comma when necessary. If necessary, look at the conversation on pages 75 and 76.

   a. Mike didn't meet Ben at the restaurant (because/so) he apologized.

   b. Mike didn't meet Ben at the restaurant (because/so) he stopped to help someone.

   c. The truck driver stopped in time (because/so) he was a good driver.

   d. The truck driver stopped in time (because/so) the truck didn't hit the woman.

   e. The woman was upset (because/so) Mike stayed with her.

   f. The woman was upset (because/so) she hurt her arm and the truck almost hit her.

   g. Ben met a woman at the restaurant (because/so) Mike said he was lucky.

   h. Ben met a woman at the restaurant (because/so) Mike didn't come.

7 Work with a partner. Ask and answer questions about the actions in the list below. Use *so* and *because* in your answers.

Example:

went to the supermarket

A: Why did you go to the supermarket?

B: I went to the supermarket because I needed some milk.

OR

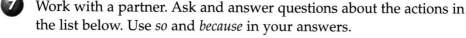

   I needed some milk, so I went to the supermarket.

a. went to the bank	**f.**	went to bed early
b. went to the hospital	**g.**	studied all weekend
c. got a new job	**h.**	took a bus
d. called the fire department	**i.**	worked out
e. bought some chocolate	**j.**	took a vacation

8 **Express Yourself** Work in groups of six. Half of you are news reporters. The other half are witnesses. You saw an emergency. Follow these steps:

- **All together:** Decide if the emergency was a fire or an accident.
- **Reporters:** Work together. Prepare your questions with *where, when, who, why, how long,* etc.
- **Witnesses:** Work together. Get ready to answer questions with *where, when, who, why, how long,* etc.
- **All together:** Reporters interview the witnesses. Take notes. Ask about details.

LISTENING and SPEAKING

Listen: A Traffic Accident

STRATEGY **1** **Before You Listen** You are going to hear a police officer and a witness talk about a traffic accident. Which words can help you understand what happened first, second, etc.? Check (✓) the words.

- ☐ while ☐ then ☐ next
- ☐ when ☐ because ☐ so

2 Listen to the conversation. What happened first, second, etc.? Number the events from 1–8.

_____ The driver of the red car saw a little dog in the intersection.

_____ The driver of the red car speeded up to get through a yellow light.

_____ The blue car drove into the red car.

_____ The driver of the red car stopped in the intersection.

_1_ A young girl was riding her bike on Clark Street.

_____ When the light turned green, the blue car speeded up.

_____ The light turned from green to yellow.

_____ The girl didn't stop for a red light at First Avenue.

Pronunciation

  Listen and repeat.

> **Linking Final Consonants to Vowels**
>
> When a final consonant sound is followed by a word that begins with a vowel, you can link the consonant to the vowel.
>
> There was an accident. The plane took off.
>
> How did it happen? We're out of time.

  Listen to the sentences. Mark the consonant-vowel link. Then practice the sentences.

Example:

A thief robbed a bank.

a. He took a lot of money.
b. He ran out the door.
c. He got on a motorcycle.
d. He hit a car.
e. He fell off the motorcycle.
f. He lost all the money.

Speak Out

STRATEGY **Disagreeing Politely** If you don't agree with someone, you can say:

> "I see what you mean, but …"   "You have a good point, but …"

 In Exercise 2 on page 81, whose fault was the accident? Was it just one person's fault? Check (✓) your opinion below. Then work with a small group. Compare and discuss your answers.

- ☐ It was the girl's fault.
- ☐ It was the dog's fault.
- ☐ It was the red car's fault.
- ☐ It was the blue car's fault.
- ☐ It was nobody's fault.

Example:

A: It was the girl's fault. She didn't stop at the red light.

B: I see what you mean, but I think it was the red car's fault.
　　　　OR
I see what you mean, but it really wasn't the girl's fault.

Read About It

 Before You Read Did you ever see a fire? What do you have to do when there's a fire?

Bed and Breakfast ... and a Fire

By Richard Suarez

[1] I was sleeping in my room at the Congress Avenue Hotel in Austin, Texas, when there was a knock on the door. Someone shouted, "Mr. Suarez! There's a fire in the hotel! Go downstairs immediately and leave the hotel. Don't wait!" I knew the voice. It was Tim Northrup, one of the owners of the hotel.

[2] I shouted an answer and quickly put on my shoes with no socks. When I opened the door, I smelled smoke! I put on my bathrobe while I was running to the stairs. There was more smoke on the stairs, but I continued down to the lobby. There, Ellen Northrup was holding a towel over her mouth and nose while she directed guests to the front door. Soon, I was standing across the street with the other guests while a hotel employee took our names and checked them off on his list. Luckily, everyone was safe.

[3] The fire department arrived very quickly. Flames were coming through the roof of the kitchen on one side of the hotel. The firefighters quickly controlled the fire and saved the main part of the hotel. Taxis arrived and took us to other hotels. And soon after that, all of my things arrived from my room at the Congress Avenue Hotel. I felt very lucky. But then I thought of the Northrups. "What will they do now?" I wondered.

[4] The Congress Avenue Hotel is a small "bed and breakfast," not a big hotel. Ellen and Tim Northrup have only twelve guest rooms in the big old house near Town Lake. Ellen cooks the big Texas-style breakfasts, and Tim serves them in the dining room. All of the guests eat together at the dining room table. It is a wonderful way to make friends when you are traveling. The Northrups love their hotel, and they make friends with all of their guests.

[5] Luckily, the Northrups saved their hotel. They built a new kitchen and opened for business again. Last week I went to stay for the weekend, and I am happy to report that the Congress Avenue Hotel is better than ever. Plan to stay there soon!

The Congress Avenue Hotel
111 Congress Avenue
Austin, Texas 78701
(512) 555-1269

STRATEGY **Understanding the Main Ideas** Each paragraph in a reading usually has one main idea. If you understand the main ideas, the reading will be clearer to you.

2 Match the main ideas with the paragraphs. Write the paragraph numbers in the blanks.

    a. Paragraph _____ is about the hotel and its owners.
    b. Paragraph _____ is about what happened outside of the hotel.
    c. Paragraphs _____ and _____ are about getting out of the hotel.
    d. Paragraph _____ is about the hotel today.

Think About It

3 Why do you think Mr. Suarez wrote "Bed and Breakfast ... and a Fire."

4 Would you like to stay in a hotel like the Congress Avenue Hotel?

Write About It

STRATEGY **5** **Before You Write** When you are a witness to an accident, you need to write down what you saw. This will help you remember important information. Make notes on a piece of paper about a real or imaginary accident or emergency. Answer the questions *When? Where? Who? What?* Do not write complete sentences. Just write the important information.

Now read this accident report.

> Last night I was walking my dog on Bay Street. At 8:25 I was in front of 1142 Bay Street. A car was going down Bay Street very fast. It hit a mini-van that was parked in front of 1131 Bay Street. The right front part of the car hit the left back part of the mini-van. The car slowed down, but then it speeded up and drove away. The car was dark blue or black. It was an old car. The license number started with AJ3 or AJ8. I didn't see everything because it was dark. The number of the mini-van was SG3-465.

6 **Write** Write a paragraph about the accident or emergency you saw. Tell what happened from the beginning to the end. Be sure to give important details.

 7 **Check Your Writing** Use the editing checklist below. Then work with a partner and check your partner's report. Discuss any questions with your partner. Revise your report if necessary.

- Did you include all the important information about the accident/emergency?
- Did you use the simple past and the past progressive correctly?
- Did you use *because* and *so* correctly?

LOVE THAT STYLE!

Unit 9

GETTING STARTED

Warm Up

1 What are the seasons in the pictures? Write *summer, fall, winter,* or *spring* under each picture.

2 Work with a partner. Look at the list of clothing. Then write each piece of clothing under the season it belongs in. You can use a word more than once.

shirt	jeans	shoes	tie	coat	umbrella
T-shirt	pants	boots	belt	hat	backpack
jacket	skirt	sandals	sunglasses	gloves	bag
sweater	leggings	sneakers	shorts	suit	swimsuit

It looks great on you!

 3 Lisa and Hannah are shopping for clothes. Listen and read.

A.

LISA: What are you looking for today?

HANNAH: I need a sweater to go with my new jeans.
I want a blue cotton sweater with a collar.
And I want it to open in the front.

LISA: Oh, nice. Do you want it with buttons or a zipper?

HANNAH: A zipper.

LISA: Long sleeves or short sleeves?

HANNAH: Long.

LISA: What size do you need?

HANNAH: Medium.

LISA: OK. You look here, and I'll look over there.

B.

LISA: Look! I found some sweaters. Do you want to try them on?

HANNAH: Oh, thanks. Let me see. No, this medium blue one isn't cotton.
It's wool.

LISA: It's just as nice as cotton.

HANNAH: Yeah, but it's too warm. And it has pockets. I don't like pockets.

LISA: OK. What about this one?

HANNAH: The light blue one? It looks worse than the first one, Lisa. It doesn't
have a zipper. It has buttons. And it has short sleeves. And look—
it's the wrong size. It's large.

LISA: Well, it isn't as expensive as the wool one. It's only twelve dollars.

HANNAH: Yeah, but I don't like it. Now, this one is better than the others.
But what *color* is that?

LISA: I don't know. Pink?

HANNAH: Hey! *This* one's nice! I love the style—long sleeves, collar, zipper.
It's perfect! And I love the color—dark blue is my favorite.

LISA: Uh, actually, I'm buying that one. It won't fit you. They only
have small.

HANNAH: You're kidding! OK. Well, I found a sweater, too. Ta-dum!
How do you like it?

LISA: I like it! It looks *great* on you! But it doesn't have a zipper or
a collar. And it's silk, not cotton. And it's red!

HANNAH: I know, but I love it! Are you ready? Let's go and pay.

C.

HANNAH:	What are *you* shopping for, Lisa?
LISA:	I have to buy a new jacket.
HANNAH:	What are you looking for? Nylon? Polyester?
LISA:	Nope—leather! My mom said I could get a black leather jacket.
HANNAH:	Oh, totally cool! You are so lucky! Let's go!

4 Circle the correct answer.

a.	Lisa and Hannah are	sisters	friends	
b.	Lisa found	two sweaters	four sweaters	a jacket
c.	Hannah found	one sweater	two sweaters	a jacket
d.	Who bought a sweater?	Lisa	Hannah	Lisa and Hannah
e.	Do you think they enjoy buying clothes?	Yes	No	

Building Vocabulary

5 **Vocabulary Check** Complete the conversation with words from the box. Use the correct form.

fit	look good	try on	zipper
go with	pockets	size	style

LISA:	I want a sweater that opens in the front.
JILL:	With buttons?
LISA:	No. I want a **(1.)** _____ .
JILL:	What **(2.)** _____ do you need?
LISA:	Large.
JILL:	Do you like this **(3.)** _____ ?
LISA:	It's OK. I like the collar, but I don't like the **(4.)** _____ .
JILL:	This shirt doesn't **(5.)** _____ me.
LISA:	You're right. It's too big. The sleeves are too long.
JILL:	Do you like this coat?
LISA:	Yeah, it **(6.)** _____ on you. How many coats did you **(7.)** _____ ?
JILL:	Four. Hey, look! This bag **(8.)** _____ my new boots.

Nouns Used as Adjectives

Some nouns can be used as adjectives to describe other nouns.

noun	*adjective* *noun*
I swim every day in the **summer**.	I like **summer** clothes.
He's learning to play **baseball**.	His **baseball** cap is red.

6 Read these sentences. Are the underlined words nouns
or adjectives? Write **N** for a noun. Write **A** for an adjective.

    a. You can't wear sandals in the <u>snow</u>. ____
       You have to wear <u>snow</u> boots. ____

    b. Carol bought sandals for her <u>spring</u> vacation. ____
       She always goes to Mexico in the <u>spring</u>. ____

    c. Maybe I'll buy a <u>leather</u> jacket. ____
       This <u>leather</u> smells good. ____

    d. The black sweater has a <u>front</u> zipper. ____
       I like sweaters that open in the <u>front</u>. ____

    e. People don't use <u>pocket</u> watches today. ____
       I like clothes with <u>pockets</u>. ____

Talk About It

7   **a.** What are your favorite clothes? Make a list of three things.
       Describe them. Think about why you like them.

    b. Work with a partner. Ask about your partner's favorite clothing.

Example:

A: What's your favorite clothing?
B: My black leather jacket. It has a lot of zippers.
A: Why do you like it?
B: Because it's so cool.

GRAMMAR

Sequence of Adjectives

When two or more adjectives come before a noun, we put them in a certain order.

	Determiner	Adjective			Noun
		Describer	**Color**	**Material**	
Luis has	two	new		cotton	shirts.
He wants	that	expensive		leather	coat.
He bought	an	ugly	green	nylon	umbrella.
He lost	his	old	brown		gloves.
Fran has	a pair of	cool	purple		sneakers.
She wants	a			silk	skirt.
She likes	my	pretty	light pink	linen	jacket.

1 Look at the chart on page 88. Circle the answers.

   a. These six words are determiners: _____.

      a   white   the   this   small   some

      red   six   her   polyester   old

   b. Describers, colors, and materials are _____.

      verbs   nouns   adjectives   determiners

   c. A material goes _____ a color.   before   after

   d. A describer goes _____ a color.   before   after

2 Work with a partner. Your partner will tell you about some clothing he or she has. Ask questions.

   Example:

A:	I have some pants.	**B:**	What material are they?
B:	Are they old or new?	**A:**	They're wool.
A:	They're old.	**B:**	So you have some old, dark
B:	What color are they?		blue, wool pants.
A:	They're dark blue.		

As + adjective + as

To say that two things are the same in some way, we can use *as* + adjective + *as*.

> The sweater is **as large as** the jacket.   The shoes are **as expensive as** the gloves.

To say that two things are different in some way, we can use *not as* + adjective + *as*.

> The T-shirt is **not as warm as** the sweater.   The shorts do **not** look **as nice as** the pants.

3 Compare the sweaters in the picture on page 86. Use the adjectives in the box. You can use the adjectives in more than one sentence. Write your sentences on a piece of paper.

   Example:

   The dark blue sweater isn't as long as the red one.

> big
> nice/cool
> long
> expensive
> small
> warm

Better than/Worse than

To say that you like one thing more or less than another, use *better than* or *worse than*.

> The purple coat **looks better than** the black one.
>
> The black coat **looks worse than** the purple one.
>
> The shoes **fit better than** the boots.

4 Wayne is helping Gary buy a jacket. Write *better than* or *worse than* on the lines.

GARY: What do you think of this green jacket, Wayne?

WAYNE: It's OK. It's **(1.)** _____ your old one.

GARY: I don't like the style. I'm going to try on this blue and white jacket. I think it'll look **(2.)** _____ the green one.

WAYNE: No, the sleeves on that jacket are too long. I think it looks **(3.)** _____ the green one.

GARY: You're right. Here's an orange one.

WAYNE: Well, it fits you **(4.)** _____ the blue and white one, but I don't think orange is a good color for you. It looks **(5.)** _____ the green one on you. Try on this blue jacket.

GARY: This jacket is too small. It fits **(6.)** _____ the blue and white one. Are there any other jackets in my size?

WAYNE: No, I don't see any. Let's go to another store.

 5 **Express Yourself** Work with a partner. Discuss these questions. What do you look for when you buy clothes? Style? Price? Fit? Color? Something else? Do you enjoy buying clothes? Why or why not?

LISTENING and SPEAKING

Listen: What Do *You* Want?

1 Do you ever buy things for people when you go on a trip? What kinds of things do you get for them?

STRATEGY **2** **Before You Listen** Carol is going on a trip to Mexico soon. She made this list of presents for her family. Do you think she's planning to buy presents for her friends? What do you think she might buy?

Mom – leather bag

Dad – shirt

Ellie and Becky – silver earrings

Ralph – CDs

3 Listen to the conversations between Carol and her friends. What else is Carol going to buy? Complete these notes.

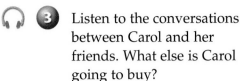

Arthur

Nicole

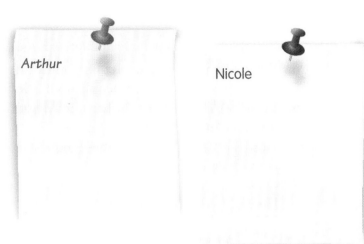

4 Read these questions. Then listen to the conversations again and circle the correct answers.

1. How does Carol sound when Arthur calls?
   a. happy   **b.** angry
2. How does Carol sound when she calls Nicole?
   a. happy   **b.** angry
3. How does Carol sound when Dave calls?
   a. happy   **b.** angry
4. Why does Carol say, "I'm so sorry!" to Dave?
   a. She made a mistake.   **b.** She has to buy many things in Mexico.

Pronunciation

> **Intonation with *or***
>
> When we ask someone to choose between two things, our voices go up before *or*, and our voices go down at the end of the question.
>
> Do you want long sleeves or short sleeves?   Do you want it with buttons *or* a zipper?

5 Listen to these questions and repeat them.
   a. Do you need medium or large?
   b. Are you going to wear a skirt or pants?
   c. Are you getting the winter coat or the rain coat?
   d. Do you like shopping in a store or buying from a catalog?
   e. Do you like the gray one or the yellow one?

Speak Out

 Asking for Opinions In a small group discussion, it is important to ask others to give their opinions. Use these expressions.

> What do you think, Carlos?   What's your opinion, Ana?
>
> Do you have an opinion on that, Katya?   What about you, Karl?

6 Discuss these questions in a small group. Ask each other for opinions.

  a. When Carol went on a trip, her family and friends asked her to buy things for them. Do people do this in your country?

  b. Carol bought presents for her family, but her friends paid her. Is it the same in your country?

  c. How did Carol feel about these requests? Why? Do you think many people would feel the same way?

  d. On a trip, did you ever have to buy a lot of things for people? How did you feel about it?

READING and WRITING

Read About It

 1 **Before You Read** The ads and the order form on pages 92–94 are from a catalog. What kinds of things do people order from catalogs? Why do people order from catalogs?

 Scanning When you are reading catalogs and order forms, look quickly at the text for the different categories (size, price, etc.) and numbers.

2 You want to order one shirt. You want to know how much shipping and handling will be. Look quickly at the shirt ad and the order form. Write the amount : $_____.

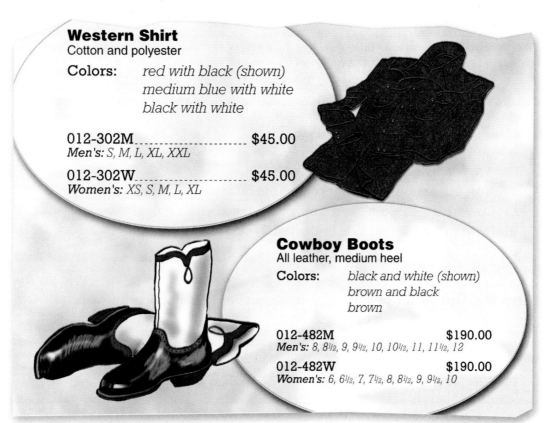

Western Shirt
Cotton and polyester

Colors: red with black (shown)
           medium blue with white
           black with white

012-302M $45.00
Men's: S, M, L, XL, XXL

012-302W $45.00
Women's: XS, S, M, L, XL

Cowboy Boots
All leather, medium heel

Colors: black and white (shown)
           brown and black
           brown

012-482M $190.00
Men's: 8, 8½, 9, 9½, 10, 10½, 11, 11½, 12

012-482W $190.00
Women's: 6, 6½, 7, 7½, 8, 8½, 9, 9½, 10

CATALOG NUMBER	NAME	SIZE	COLOR	PRICE
012-302M	Western Shirt	XL	blue/white	45.00
012-482M	Cowboy boots	11	brown/black	190.00
012-482W	Cowboy boots	8	black/white	190.00
			SUBTOTAL	425.00
			SHIPPING & HANDLING	13.00
			TOTAL	$438.00

ORDER FORM

COWBOYS & COWGIRLS
WESTERN WEAR, INC.
800 CIRCLE ROAD
CONROY, WYOMING 82400
USA

SHIPPING AND HANDLING

Under $50 total Add $5
Under $100 total Add $8
Under $200 total Add $11
$200 + Add $13

✓Mr. Mrs. Miss. Marion Stanley
Street Address 10055 Madrid Drive
City Los Angeles **State or Province** CA
Zip/Postal Code 90103 **Country** USA
Phone with Area Code: (213) 555-9684
Credit Card Number (or send check or money order): _____
Expiration Date: _____

---

3 Read the ads and the order form in Exercise 2. Circle the correct answers.

1. What important information is in the catalog but not on the order form?
   a. price b. size and color c. style and material

2. "XL" means ____ .
   a. small or medium b. extra large c. extra extra large

3. In the catalog number, "M" means ____ .
   a. men's b. medium

4. Marion Stanley is a ____ .
   a. man b. woman

5. Which item on the order form is Marion Stanley not going to wear?
   a. the shirt b. the brown and black boots c. the black and white boots

6. Marion Stanley paid by ____ .
   a. credit card b. check or money order

Write About It

4 You can order from a catalog by telephone or by mail. Catalogs include a mail order form, but sometimes the form is not there and you need to write a letter. Sally Marsh ordered boots. Read her letter.

```
2246 East Second Street                    June 11, 2000
Hometown, Wisconsin 54173


Cowboys and Cowgirls Western Wear, Inc.
800 Circle Drive
Conroy, Wyoming 82400


       Please send me one pair of cowboy boots, size 10,
in brown.  The catalog number is 012-482W.  I am sending
you $201.00, which includes shipping and handling.


Thank you.

Sally Marsh
```

5 Before You Write You are going to write a letter to order some jeans from Cowboys and Cowgirls Western Wear, Inc. Look at this ad and the order form on page 93. Circle the information on the form that you will need to include in your letter.

Western Jeans
All cotton, traditional fit, western style

Colors: dark blue (shown)
              light blue
              black
              white

012-298M $30.00
Men's: 30, 32, 34, 36, 38, 40, 42, 44

012-298W $30.00
Women's: 4, 6, 8, 10, 12, 14, 16, 18

6 Write Write your letter. Order as many pairs of jeans as you want. Make sure you include all the necessary information so that they can send you the jeans.

7 Check Your Writing Answer the questions below. Check your partner's letter. Discuss any questions with your partner. Revise your letter if necessary.

- Did you include all the necessary information?
- Are your numbers correct?
- Did you use the correct form for your letter?

1 Complete each sentence with the noun in parentheses. If necessary, add *a/an* before the noun or *s* after the noun.

   a. Elena ate three **(piece)** _____ of pizza.

   b. My brother can't drink **(milk)** _____ .

   c. Do you want **(sandwich)** _____ ? I have an extra one.

   d. Trish doesn't like **(coffee)** _____ .

   e. Please get some **(vegetable)** _____ at the store.

   f. I always eat **(apple)** _____ after dinner.

2 Read these sentences with nonspecific quantities. Cross out the word or words that you can't use.

   a. How much/many milk do we have?

   b. We had some/any/a little milk this morning.

   c. We don't have any/a little/a lot of grapes.

   d. How much/many carrots are there in the refrigerator?

   e. I need some/a lot of/a few garlic for the salad.

   f. Lucy always has a few/a lot of/any cookies after lunch.

3 Read these sentences with specific quantities. Cross out the word or words that you can't use.

   a. I'd like two pounds/a bunch/a carton of those bananas, please.

   b. I bought a quart/a bag/a package of cookies for dessert.

   c. I ate a can/a serving/a bunch of beans.

   d. Can you please buy a can/a cup/a half kilo of tuna?

   e. Could I have a glass/a liter/a kilo of milk, please?

   f. I need a half pound/two cups/a bunch of sugar for this recipe.

4 Complete the sentences with the determiners and adjectives in parentheses. Put the words in the correct order.

   a. Ruby decided to buy **(red/expensive/an/leather)** _____ coat.

   b. Leon has **(silk/or/great/five/six)** _____ shirts from Hong Kong.

   c. These shoes are better than **(the/brown/old/ugly)** _____ ones I wore last week.

   d. My father lets me wear **(purple/wool/old/his/and/orange)** _____ baseball jacket.

   e. She always buys **(a/flat/white/pair/of)** _____ summer sandals in June.

5 Rewrite each pair of sentences as one sentence. Do not change the order of the sentences. Use *when, while, because,* or *so* in the middle of the new sentence (not at the beginning).

a. On Sunday night, we were reading in bed. We heard someone at the door.

b. I went to the door. Harry was looking for his bathrobe.

c. Our neighbor, Sam, wanted to use our phone. His phone wasn't working.

d. Sam needed to call his mother. He always calls her on Sunday night.

e. I was making tea. Sam was talking to his mother.

f. I was waiting for the tea. I looked out of the window at Sam's house.

g. There were flames in Sam's house! I shouted to Sam and pointed out the window!

h. Sam had to call the fire department. He said good-bye to his mother—fast!

Vocabulary Review

Complete the conversations with the words from the box. Use the correct forms.

a catalog	to order
a vegetable	a vegetarian
on	to fit
to fall	to miss
lucky	with
to have	upset
to hurt	to break
to taste	to forget

1. **LOUIE:** That suit looks good **(1.)** _____ you.

DEWEY: Really? It doesn't **(2.)** _____ me very well. I **(3.)** _____ it from **(4.)** _____ .

LOUIE: Can't you send it back?

DEWEY: Not now. I wore it to a wedding. My girlfriend was really **(5.)** _____ .

LOUIE: Why?

DEWEY: It was our wedding.

2. **SALLY:** What happened?

SANDY: I **(6.)** _____ downstairs and **(7.)** _____ my back. But I was **(8.)** _____ . Your bicycle was at the bottom of the stairs and **(9.)** I _____ it.

SALLY: Well, that's good! It's a new bicycle. I'm glad you didn't **(10.)** _____ it.

3. **ELLA:** Hi. Come and **(11.)** _____ this. Does it need salt?

FRED: Hmm. It's … interesting. What's in it?

ELLA: Beans, spices, ground beef …

FRED: Beef? Ugh! You know I'm a **(12.)** _____ .

ELLA: Oops! Sorry. I **(13.)** _____ .

Unit
10

a. _____

b. _____

c. _____

d. _____

e. _____

f. _____

g. _____

GETTING STARTED

Warm Up

1 Write the kind of transportation under each picture.

bike	train	plane
motorcycle	boat	car
bus		

2 Write the vacation sights under each picture.

beach	ocean	forest	mountains
island	river	zoo	museum

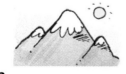

a. _____

b. _____

c. _____

d. _____

e. _____

f. _____

g. _____

h. _____

3 Work with a partner. Ask and answer questions about your vacation plans.

Example:

A: Where do you want to go on your vacation?

B: I want to go to the beach.

A: How are you going to get there?

B: By car.

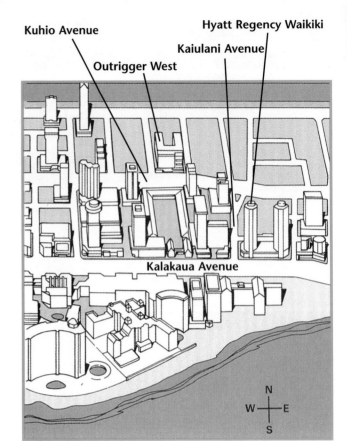

Kuhio Avenue
Hyatt Regency Waikiki
Kaiulani Avenue
Outrigger West
Kalakaua Avenue

What a surprise!

4 Listen and read.

TYLER: Greg! What a surprise!

GREG: Hey! Tyler! What are you doing in Honolulu?

TYLER: I'm here on vacation with my family.

GREG: Me, too. We're staying at the Hyatt Regency Waikiki.

TYLER: I know where that is. We're staying at the Outrigger West. It's not very far from you.

GREG: Oh, really? Where is it?

TYLER: It's near the International Market Place.

TYLER: What are you doing this afternoon? Maybe we can get together and go sightseeing.

GREG: Sorry, I can't go today. The sailing instructor at the hotel is going to give me a sailing lesson. It's included in the price, so I don't want to miss it. Are you doing anything tomorrow?

TYLER: Yeah, we're taking a boat trip to another island. How about Wednesday morning? I'll be free then.

GREG: Wednesday's great. Where do you want to meet?

TYLER: How about my hotel?

GREG: Fine. How do I get there?

TYLER: Here's a map. Let's see. From the Hyatt Regency, you walk north on Kaiulani Avenue to Kuhio Avenue. Turn left and go about one block. The hotel will be on your right—the Outrigger West.

GREG: North on Kaiulani and then west on Kuhio. Is 9:30 OK?

TYLER: That's fine. I'll be in the lobby at 9:30.

5 Answer the questions. Use complete sentences.

a. Where are Tyler and Greg?

b. Why are they surprised to see each other?

c. Why aren't they meeting this afternoon or tomorrow?

d. When are they meeting? Where?

e. Find their hotels on the map. Draw a line where Greg will walk.

Building Vocabulary

Reading a Map

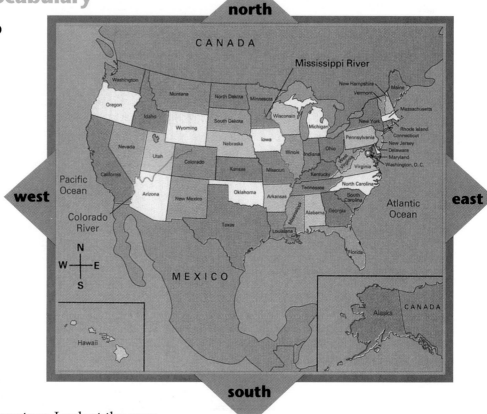

6 Work with a partner. Look at the map of the United States. Complete the statements.

  a. Nevada is in the _____.
  b. Minnesota is in the _____.
  c. Pennsylvania is in the _____.
  d. Louisiana is in the _____.
  e. Hawaii is a group of _____.
  f. California, Arizona, New Mexico, and Texas are north of _____.
  g. The _____ is east of the United States.
  h. Washington, Oregon, and California are next to the _____.
  i. The _____ goes through the United States from north to south.
  j. The _____ begins in Colorado and goes southwest.

Expressions with *Go* + Verb + *–ing*

To talk about sports and recreation, we often use the expression *go* + verb *–ing*.

We **go bowling** every Saturday.	I**'m going fishing** tomorrow.
He **went swimming** in the lake.	**Can** we **go shopping**?
biking dancing	jogging shopping
bowling fishing	rollerblading sightseeing
camping hiking	sailing swimming

7 Complete the letter. Use expressions from the box on page 99. Be sure to use the correct form of the verb.

Dear Joanna,

We're having a wonderful time. This morning, we put on our sneakers and **(1.)** _____ in the park. Later, we rented a sailboat and **(2.)** _____ on the lake. The water was warm, so we **(3.)** _____, too. Then we **(4.)** _____ in the city. We saw the art museum and walked around in the old part of the city. There were some stores near the museum, so we **(5.)** _____. I bought T-shirts for everybody at home. Tonight we're going to **(6.)** _____ at a club. Tomorrow we're going to rent bicycles and **(7.)** _____ in the mountains. I'll tell you all about it when I get home.

Emily

Talk About It

8 Study the map. Then work with a partner. One of you asks for directions, and the other one gives them. Take turns.

Example:

A: I'm at the library. How do I get to the theater?

B: Walk east on Ohio Avenue to Second Street. Turn right on Second. Then walk south for about one block. It's just south of the Chinese restaurant.

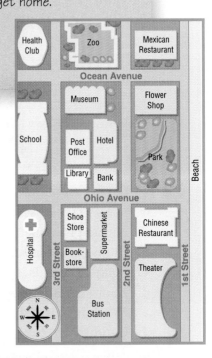

GRAMMAR

The Present Progressive: Future Meaning

We can use the present progressive tense to talk about future plans. The meaning is the same as *be going to* + verb. We usually use a time expression to show the future meaning.

A:	What **are** you **doing** on Friday afternoon?
B:	I**'m working** late this Friday.
A:	I**'m going shopping** on Saturday. Do you want to come with me?
B:	Thanks, but I**'m going camping** this weekend.

1 Read each sentence and decide if it is about the present or the future. Check (✓) the correct box.

		Present	Future
a.	I'm studying English this year.	☐	☐
b.	I'm studying English next year, too.	☐	☐
c.	I'm eating lunch with Ben tomorrow.	☐	☐
d.	I'm eating lunch now.	☐	☐
e.	I'm leaving now.	☐	☐
f.	I'm leaving for New York on Tuesday.	☐	☐

2 Work with a partner. Take turns asking and answering questions about your future plans. Use the time expressions in the box.

tomorrow night	Thursday afternoon	Friday night
Wednesday morning	Thursday evening	Saturday morning

Example:

A: What are you doing tomorrow afternoon?
B: I'm playing tennis.

Clauses with *If*

We use *if* clauses to show possible results.

What will Jane do if she feels sick tomorrow?	
If she feels sick, she will stay at the hotel.	She will stay at the hotel **if she feels sick.**
If she is sick, she won't go to the beach.	She won't go to the beach **if she is sick.**
If she doesn't feel well, she'll stay in bed.	She'll stay in bed **if she doesn't feel well.**

 When the *if* clause is at the beginning of the sentence, use a comma.

3 Claudia is going on a business trip. Her brother, Eduardo, is going to take care of her children. She's telling him what to expect. Write sentences with *if*. Use the cues on page 102.

Example:

the baby get hungry / he cry
If the baby gets hungry, he'll cry.

the kids be happy / you buy ice cream
The kids will be happy if you buy ice cream.

a. the baby be happy/you give him his bottle
b. the kids watch TV/they be quiet
c. they have nothing to do/they get bored
d. they run around the house/they get bored
e. they run around the house/they break things
f. I be at the Downtown Hotel/you want to call me
g. you leave me a message/I call you back
h. I be really grateful/you do this for me

 4 Express Yourself

a. Complete this calendar for next week. Write the month at the top of the page. Write the dates beside the days. Write five things that you are doing next week and the times you are doing them.

b. Work with a partner. Ask your partner to do something with you. Talk about where and when you can meet. Then give directions on how to get to the meeting place.

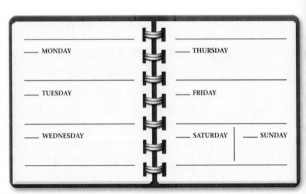

LISTENING and SPEAKING

Listen: When Can We Get Together?

1 Did you ever visit someone in another city? Did you go sightseeing? What did you see?

 2 Before You Listen You're going to hear a telephone conversation between Lee and Pat. They are friends. Lee lives in New York. Pat is visiting relatives in New York. Look at the title above and the chart in Exercise 3 below. What do you think Lee and Pat will talk about?

 3 Listen to the conversation. Check (✓) the name of the person who is going to do each activity.

Lee	Pat		Wed	Thur	Fri	Sat	Sun
✓		a. go to an appointment					
		b. have a family dinner					
		c. see a Broadway show					
		d. have a class					
		e. go to a wedding					
		f. take a boat trip					

 4 Listen again. Check the day when each activity is going to happen.

Pronunciation

> **Thought Groups**
>
> When we speak, we don't stop between every word. We speak in phrases or groups of words that express a thought.
>
> He arrived in the morning.
>
> If you call me before you leave, I'll be ready.

  5 Listen to these sentences. Then read them aloud. The thought groups are marked.

    a. If we go to Washington, D.C., we'll take the train.

    b. Washington State is in the northwest of the United States.

    c. When I go on vacation, I like to eat in small restaurants.

    d. If we have time, we'll go swimming.

    e. Bob lives on an island in the Pacific Ocean.

    f. We're staying at the Regency Park Hotel in Miami.

Speak Out

 Convincing Someone of a Plan To convince someone to agree with you, give a reason why your plan is better.

> In Hawaii, you can go swimming every day.
>
> If we stay near the beach, it'll be quiet.

 6 Work with a partner. You have just won a vacation trip! Someone is going to pay for your vacation, but you and your partner have to go together. Where do you want to go? What do you want to do? Plan your trip. Convince your partner that your plan is better.

READING and WRITING

Read About It

 Before You Read Look at the two brochures on page 104. What kind of information do you often find in brochures?

Scanning When you want specific information from a text, read quickly and look for the necessary details.

2 Scan the brochures to answer the questions below. Check the correct boxes.

Which vacation ...	Club Pacific	Island Tour
... is ten days?	☐	☐
... visits two islands?	☐	☐
... offers windsurfing and sailing?	☐	☐
... offers camping on the beach?	☐	☐

HAVE THE TIME OF YOUR LIFE AT
CLUB PACIFIC

Enjoy ten days and nights at **CLUB PACIFIC** for the perfect Hawaiian vacation! More luxury, more excitement, more things to do!

See Honolulu with other fun, interesting people. **CLUB PACIFIC** gives you a free tour of the city in a luxurious bus with an expert guide!

Learn windsurfing, waterskiing, or sailing. **CLUB PACIFIC** gives you four free lessons with an expert teacher!

Dance the night away in our exciting dance club with internationally famous bands!

Visit beautiful Kauai island for delicious Hawaiian food at a real Hawaiian luau.

Work out in our new 24-hour health club! Free for guests of **CLUB PACIFIC!**

Relax and watch the ocean at breakfast in your large, luxurious room. At **CLUB PACIFIC**, all rooms have ocean views. And breakfast is free!

And **CLUB PACIFIC** also has three restaurants, two swimming pools, a post office, and many wonderful shops!

Call your travel agent today!

Get Back to Nature in Hawaii!
The Island Tour Vacation

If you're looking for a simple, natural vacation, you'll love **The Island Tour!** Most people see only the big city of Honolulu on the main island of Oahu. On **The Island Tour,** you get ten days of camping and hiking on two of the other islands—Hawaii and Kauai.

On Hawaii ...

Climb a mountain in the Hawaiian Volcanoes National Park.

Relax on Hawaii's famous beaches and swim in the blue water of the Pacific Ocean.

On Kauai ...

Enjoy nature while you take a boat trip on the Huleia River.

Hike through the forest in beautiful Waimea Canyon.

On **The Island Tour,** you camp on the beach—and you never have to think about money! One price covers everything, including all food, your guide, and transportation for ten days. For a vacation you'll never forget ...

Call us today at 800-555-1222.

③ **Vocabulary Check** Match the words and expressions from the brochures with their meanings. Write the letters next to the numbers.
"CP" = Club Pacific Reading "IT" = Island Tour reading

_____ **1.** luxurious (CP)	**a.** to walk up
_____ **2.** expert (CP)	**b.** to include
_____ **3.** guide (CP, IT)	**c.** a person who knows a lot about a topic
_____ **4.** view (CP)	**d.** what you can see
_____ **5.** nature (IT)	**e.** with nothing extra
_____ **6.** simple (IT)	**f.** a person who shows you interesting things
_____ **7.** to climb (IT)	**g.** to stay without a house or hotel
_____ **8.** to hike (IT)	**h.** forest, mountains, lakes, rivers
_____ **9.** to camp (IT)	**i.** expensive, nice, but not necessary
_____ **10.** to cover (IT)	**j.** to walk for a long time, outside the city

④ Check (✓) what's included in the price of each vacation.

	Club Pacific	Island Tour			Club Pacific	Island Tour
1. hotel	☐	☐		**7.** city tour	☐	☐
2. transportation	☐	☐		**8.** boat trip	☐	☐
3. breakfast	☐	☐		**9.** guide	☐	☐
4. lunch	☐	☐		**10.** lessons	☐	☐
5. dinner	☐	☐		**11.** health club	☐	☐
6. luau	☐	☐				

Think About It

⑤ Which vacation would you prefer to go on—
Club Pacific or Island Tour? Why?
In a small group, discuss your preferences.

Write About It

6 Invitations tell your guests who, what, when, where, and sometimes why. Maps and directions need to give only helpful information, with nothing extra. Read the invitation and the directions. Study the map.

Dear Nancy,
We're having a party! No special reason—just for fun! Please come, and bring a friend if you want to.

Date: Saturday, August 24th
Time: 8:00 p.m.
Place: 33 Park Street
RSVP: By August 18th (Please!)
Phone: 882-9966

All the best!
Tom

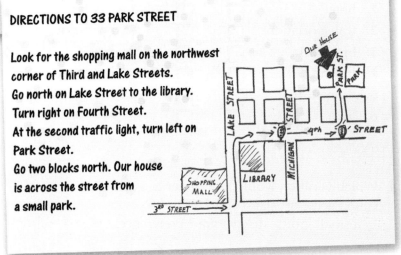

DIRECTIONS TO 33 PARK STREET

Look for the shopping mall on the northwest corner of Third and Lake Streets.
Go north on Lake Street to the library.
Turn right on Fourth Street.
At the second traffic light, turn left on Park Street.
Go two blocks north. Our house is across the street from a small park.

 STRATEGY

 7 **Before You Write** You are going to have a party at your home or school. What information do you need to include in the invitation and the directions? Make notes.

 8 **Write** Write the invitation. Then draw a map and write the directions.

 9 **Check Your Writing** Use the questions below to check your work. Revise your invitation, map, or directions if necessary.

- Will people have all the information they need about the party?
- Will they be able to reply?
- Will they be able to find the place?

ART FOR ART'S SAKE

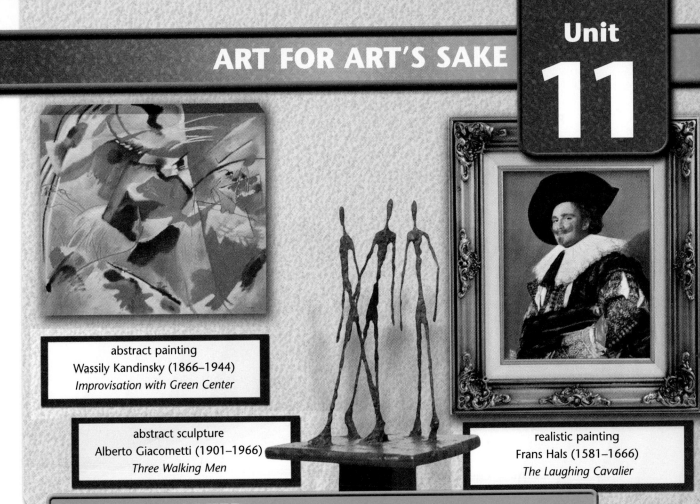

abstract painting
Wassily Kandinsky (1866–1944)
Improvisation with Green Center

abstract sculpture
Alberto Giacometti (1901–1966)
Three Walking Men

realistic painting
Frans Hals (1581–1666)
The Laughing Cavalier

GETTING STARTED

Warm Up

1 Work with a partner. Ask and answer the questions. Do you and your partner agree or disagree?

a. Where do you usually see art? In museums? In people's homes? In parks? In schools? Where else?

b. In general, do you prefer abstract art or realistic art?

c. Do you prefer painting, sculpture, or photography?

d. Do you have a favorite artist? Who is it? Why do you like him/her?

I think those seats are ours.

 2 Listen and read.

A. **MARY:** There you are! What happened?

SETH: I'm sorry I'm late. First, I couldn't find my keys. Then there was a lot of traffic and the bus had to go really slowly.

MARY: Well, don't worry about it. I have our tickets. Let's go in and find our seats.

B.

MARY: Let's see. We're in row P, seats 16 and 18.

SETH: Here's row P. And here's seat 14.

MARY: Those two seats have to be ours, but there are people sitting in them … Excuse me, I think those seats are ours.

PLAYGOER: Sorry, they can't be yours. We always sit here.

MARY: But our tickets say 16 and 18. Are you sure …

SETH: Excuse me, Mary. Those tickets say row F.

MARY: Oh, I'm so sorry! I read it wrong. I guess I need reading glasses.

PLAYGOER: That's OK.

C.

SETH: There are our seats … right in the middle. Excuse me. Sorry to disturb you.

MARY: Excuse me. Oh, sorry! Excuse me, please. Whew! Here we are! And it's only five minutes to eight.

SETH: Good, we have a few minutes. I want to read about this play. Do you have my program?

MARY: No, they only gave me one. Whose program is that? Isn't it yours?

SETH: No, it's hers—the woman sitting next to me.

MARY: Well, here, you can read mine.

SETH: That's OK. I'll go and get one.

MARY: Well, you'd better go fast. It's going to start.

SETH: I know. I'll be right back. Excuse me. Excuse me, please …

3 Read the statements. Write **T** for true or **F** for false.

a. _____ Seth was late because he missed the bus.

b. _____ There were people sitting in their seats.

c. _____ There were people sitting in their row.

d. _____ They went to a concert.

e. _____ It probably started at eight o'clock.

f. _____ Seth didn't have a program, but Mary had hers.

g. _____ Seth wanted to read Mary's program.

h. _____ Mary went to get a program for Seth.

Building Vocabulary

  4 **Vocabulary Check** Find words or expressions in the three conversations that match the meanings below. Write them on the lines.

a. That's OK. (Part A) _____

b. chairs in a theater (Parts A, B) _____

c. line of seats (Part B) _____

d. center (Part C) _____

e. bother (Part C) _____

f. return very soon (Part C) _____

g. you need to (Part C) _____

h. description of a performance (Part C) _____

I'm sorry and *Excuse me*

We use *I'm sorry* and *Excuse me* in several different ways.

Apologizing

I'm sorry I hurt your feelings.

Sorry! (I stepped on your foot.)

Excuse me! (I sneezed.)

Excuse me! (I need to get past you.)

Interrupting or getting someone's attention

Excuse me. Could I say something?

Excuse me. Can you help me?

Disagreeing

I'm sorry, but I think you're wrong.

Excuse me! That's wrong.

---

5 Find examples of *I'm sorry* and *Excuse me* in the conversations and underline them. Write the letter **(a–d)** next to each kind of example.

a. Apologizing to someone (find three examples)

b. Getting someone's attention (find one example)

c. Interrupting someone (find one example)

d. Disagreeing with someone (find one example)

Talk About It

 6 Work in small groups. Your city wants to buy a sculpture to put in front of the library. Two groups, a group of artists and a group of citizens, selected three possible sculptures. Now your job is to make the final selection.

Look at the information on page 110 about each sculpture. Which sculpture will you choose? Why? After you choose, work with another group. Compare your choices and reasons.

Sculptor: Emma Jackson, new artist
Type: Abstract sculpture called "Reading"
Price: $60,000
Artists' group: 70% prefer it.
Citizens' group: 20% prefer it.

Sculptor: Paul Morton, artist from your city
Type: Realistic sculpture of a famous writer who lived in your city
Price: $85,000
Artists' group: 10% prefer it.
Citizens' group: 50% prefer it.

Sculptor: Rosina Correlli, famous artist
Type: Realistic sculpture of a father reading to his young daughter
Price: $200,000
Artists' group: 20% prefer it.
Citizens' group: 30% prefer it.

GRAMMAR

Whose and Possessive Pronouns

We use *whose* + noun to ask who something belongs to. We use possessive pronouns to tell who something belongs to.

Whose painting is this? I like it.	It's **mine**. But it isn't as good as **yours**.
Whose painting is that?	It's **hers**. It's better than **ours**.

Possessive Pronouns:

my	—	mine	our	— ours
your	—	yours	your	— yours
his	—	his	their	— theirs
her	—	hers		
it	—	its		

1 Choose the correct words to complete the three conversations. Write them in the spaces.

Tom: (1. Who/Whose) _____ car keys are these?
Pavel: Maybe they belong to John. He was just here.
Tom: I'm sure they're not (2. him/his) _____ . He doesn't drive.
Pavel: Wait a minute! Let me see them. I think they're (3. my/mine) _____ . I usually keep (4. my/mine) _____ keys in my pocket, but they aren't there now.

JULIO: Aren't these seats **(5. our/ours)** _____?

KIM: No, they're **(6. their/theirs)** _____. I see **(7. our/ours)** _____ seats. They're in the next row.

MARK: Look at that woman over there. Her briefcase looks just like **(8. your/yours)** _____.

SALLY: That briefcase isn't **(9. her/hers)** _____. It's **(10. mine/my)** _____!

Adverbs

Adverbs tell us how someone does something.

Adjective	Adverb
Tony and Pete are careful workers.	They work very **carefully**.
Carol is often angry.	She spoke to me **angrily** this morning.
Yoko is a fast walker.	She walks too **fast** for me.
My brother is a good photographer.	He photographs animals **well**.

Many adverbs are formed by adding –ly to the adjective.

Adjective	Adverb	Adjective	Adverb
bad	badly	easy	easily
beautiful	beautifully	happy	happily
quiet	quietly	terrible	terribly
angry	angrily	comfortable	comfortably

Some adverbs are irregular.

Adjective	Adverb	Adjective	Adverb
fast	fast	wrong	wrong
hard	hard	good	well

2 Complete the chart.

Adjective	Adverb	Adjective	Adverb
a. *enthusiastic*	enthusiastically	**f.** kind	
b. competitive		**g.**	responsibly
c.	sloppily	**h.** careful	
d. confident		**i.**	carelessly
e.	greedily	**j.** slow	

3 Work with a partner. Ask and answer questions about Jack. Use adverbs in your answers.

Example: Jack is a careless writer.

A: How does Jack write?
B: He writes carelessly.

a. Jack is a slow walker.
b. Jack is a hard worker.
c. Jack is a good actor.
d. Jack is a careful painter.
e. Jack is a dangerous driver.

f. Jack is a bad speller.
g. Jack is a fast swimmer.
h. Jack is a clear speaker.
i. Jack is a loud singer.
j. Jack is a fashionable dresser.

4 Choose three roles in the box. Describe yourself in each of those roles. On a piece of paper, write two sentences with adverbs for each role.

student	writer
singer	driver
worker	athlete
cook	dancer

Examples:

Student: *I study hard. I learn things quickly.*

Singer: *I sing loudly. I don't sing very well.*

 5 **Express Yourself** Work with a partner. Look at the roles your partner circled in Exercise 4 above. Ask your partner questions about the three roles. Answer your partner's questions.

Example:

A: What kind of student are you?
B: I study hard and I learn things quickly. What kind of singer are you?
A: Well, I sing loudly, but I don't sing well.

LISTENING and SPEAKING

Listen: Are You Serious?

1 Do you like to look at art? Do you prefer to look at it alone or with friends? Do you enjoy discussing art with your friends?

Guiseppe Arcimboldo
(1527–1593)
Summer (Allegory)

Pablo Picasso (1881–1973)
Weeping Woman

2 **Before You Listen** It is easier to understand a conversation when you already know something about the topic. Look at the two pictures on page 112. In what ways are they realistic? In what ways are they abstract?

 3 Listen to this conversation among three friends—David, Carla, and Sandy. Which painting does each person prefer? In the chart, circle **P** for the Picasso; circle **A** for the Arcimboldo. If a person does not like the paintings at all, circle **X**.

Person	Painting			Why?
David	P	A	X	
Carla	P	A	X	
Sandy	P	A	X	

 4 Listen again. Why does each person feel that way? Write the answers in the chart.

Pronunciation

Reductions

In normal speech, we often reduce and link sounds so that two or more words sound like one. For example:

"Where did you go?" is often pronounced as /wɛrdjə go/.

 5 Listen to the sentences. Circle the words that together sound like one word.

Example:
(Where did you) go?

a. Did you eat lunch?
b. Does your sister work here?
c. I thought you were coming.
d. What's your brother doing?

e. Would you like an apple?
f. That's your suitcase.
g. Aren't you going to visit me?
h. Is your friend still sick?

 6 Listen again and repeat the sentences.

Speak Out

STRATEGY **Disagreeing Strongly** If you are talking with friends, you don't always have to be as polite. You can use these expressions to disagree strongly.

Come on, (Keiko). That's crazy!

Excuse me! Are you serious?

7 Work with a small group. Discuss the two paintings by Picasso and Arcimboldo. What do you like about them? What don't you like?

Example:

A: Which one do you like?

B: I prefer the Arcimboldo.

A: Why?

B: Because he paints so beautifully. Everything is so perfect.

C: Excuse me! Are you serious? It's a person made out of fruit. How can you like it?

READING and WRITING

Read About It

 Before You Read Look at the pictures and read the title. Do you know anything about the painters? What do you think the article is about?

Changing Ideas About Art

A lot of modern art is not realistic or beautiful. Artists want to show people a different way of seeing things. They want to say something about the world they live in. Modern paintings and sculptures disturb some people because they
5 do not like or understand what the artist is trying to express. It often takes many years before an artist's work is accepted by the public.

In 1870, Vincent van Gogh and Claude Monet were painting in France. They and some other painters shared
10 many ideas about art. They used strong, bright colors, and their pictures weren't always very realistic. Their art was very different from what people were familiar with, and few people liked it. The group did not make a lot of money with their paintings. Van Gogh sold only one painting while he
15 was alive.

Today, we call this group the Impressionists. Van Gogh's and Monet's paintings sell for millions of dollars and Impressionist paintings are in museums all over the world. The Impressionists are not only respected, they are also
20 popular. People everywhere buy their work in inexpensive posters and prints. When museums have special exhibits of Impressionist paintings, people stand in line patiently for hours to get in.

Artists' ideas change quickly, but the public's ideas change much more slowly. Generally, artists who are truly popular in their lifetimes are not well respected. Those
25 who are respected can become rich, but they are seldom popular. Most of today's new artists will be forgotten in 100 years. Only a few of them will be immortal.

Claude Monet
(1840–1926)
Water Lilies

Vincent van Gogh
(1853–1890)
The Artist's Bedroom at Arles

Vocabulary Check Use the context to match the words from the article with the correct meanings.

1. _____ disturb (line 4)
2. _____ express (line 5)
3. _____ public (line 7)
4. _____ shared ideas (line 9–10)
5. _____ familiar with (line 12)
6. _____ popular (line 20)
7. _____ exhibits (line 21)
8. _____ immortal (line 26)

a. recognize
b. shows
c. upset
d. undying
e. liked by many people
f. had similar thoughts
g. say
h. people

STRATEGY **Understanding Reference Words** Good writers use many words like *they, their, this,* and *those.* If you can understand what these words refer to, you will understand the reading much better.

 In the article, what do these words mean? Circle the correct answer.

1. *they* (line 2)
   a. artists
   b. people
   c. things
2. *they* (line 4)
   a. some people
   b. artists
   c. painting and sculptures
3. *what* (line 5)
   a. the people that
   b. the artists that
   c. the art that
4. *their* (line 11)
   a. people's
   b. the group's
   c. Van Gogh's and Monet's
5. *those* (line 24)
   a. artists
   b. the public
   c. the Impressionists
6. *them* (line 26)
   a. today's new artists
   b. artists in 2100
   c. the Impressionists

Think About It

 Read these statements by two artists—a composer and a painter. What do you think they mean? Do you agree or disagree? Explain.

"If it is art, it is not for all, and if it is for all, it is not art."
—*Arnold Schoenberg*

"Art is meant to disturb."
—*Georges Braque*

Write About It

STRATEGY **5** **Before You Write** Personal e-mail letters are usually very simple. They are often very short, and they sometimes don't have a greeting or a signature. Read Henry's e-mail letter to his friend Jeff. Why did he write the letter? Did he include any other information?

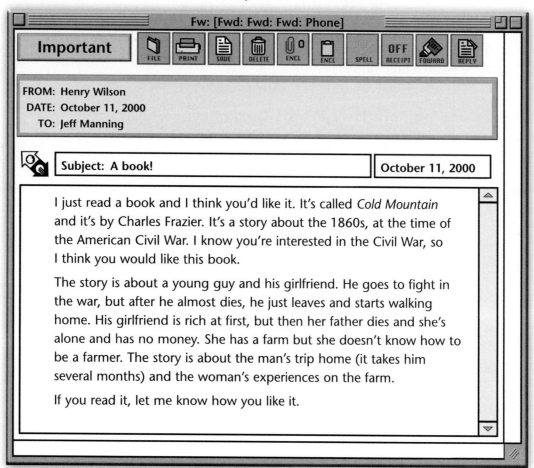

Fw: [Fwd: Fwd: Fwd: Phone]

Important
FILE PRINT SAVE DELETE ENCL ENCL SPELL OFF RECEIPT FOWARD REPLY

FROM: Henry Wilson
DATE: October 11, 2000
TO: Jeff Manning

Subject: A book! | October 11, 2000

I just read a book and I think you'd like it. It's called *Cold Mountain* and it's by Charles Frazier. It's a story about the 1860s, at the time of the American Civil War. I know you're interested in the Civil War, so I think you would like this book.

The story is about a young guy and his girlfriend. He goes to fight in the war, but after he almost dies, he just leaves and starts walking home. His girlfriend is rich at first, but then her father dies and she's alone and has no money. She has a farm but she doesn't know how to be a farmer. The story is about the man's trip home (it takes him several months) and the woman's experiences on the farm.

If you read it, let me know how you like it.

6 **Write** Think of a movie or a book that you would like to recommend to a friend. Write an e-mail message to your friend.

- Write *From, Date, To,* and *Subject,* as in Henry's e-mail.

- In the first paragraph, give the name of the book or movie. If it's a book, give the author's name, too. Then tell your friend why he or she would like it.

- In the second paragraph, give a little information about the book or movie, but don't tell the ending! If it's a story, you can use the present tense.

7 **Check Your Writing** Check your e-mail letter. Use the editing checklist below. Revise your letter if necessary.

- Is your letter simple and easy to understand?
- Will your friend want to read the book or see the movie?
- Is your spelling correct?

WHAT'S THE MATTER?

Unit 12

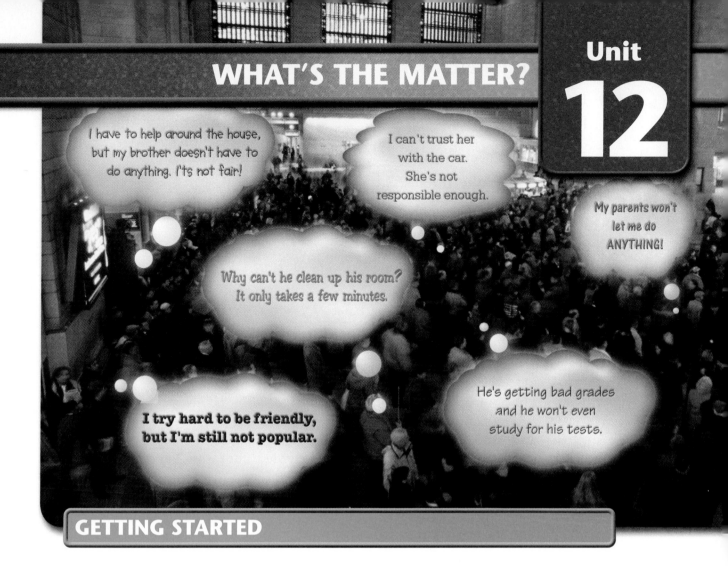

GETTING STARTED

Warm Up

 Work with a partner. Answer the questions.

a. Look at the picture. Which things do you think teenagers said? Which things do you think parents said?

b. What other things do teenagers complain about? What else do they worry about? Make a list.

c. What other things do parents complain about? What else do they worry about? Make a list.

She's driving me crazy!

 2 Listen and read.

JERRY: My sister is driving me crazy!

RITA: What do you mean?

JERRY: She's always taking my things. Yesterday she took my bike. I looked out the window, and she was riding away on it. I had to walk to my soccer game.

RITA: Did you talk to her about it?

JERRY: Yeah, I told her to stop taking my things.

RITA: What did she say?

JERRY: She got mad and shouted at me. She said she asked me for permission, and I said OK.

RITA: Did you?

JERRY: No. I didn't even hear her. I guess I nodded, but I wasn't nodding at her. I was talking on the phone.

RITA: Did you explain that to her?

JERRY: Sure. But she didn't want to listen. She said her bike had a flat tire and she needed to go to her baby-sitting job. She said her job was far away and my soccer game was near here.

RITA: Well, that doesn't sound so bad.

JERRY: Yeah, well, *then* she said I only think about myself and not about other people. She says I'm her brother and I should help her.

RITA: Does she ever help *you?*

JERRY: No.

RITA: So why don't you ask her to help you with something?

JERRY: That's good advice. Maybe I'll ask her to help me with French.

RITA: There's something else you can do, too.

JERRY: What?

RITA: You can help her fix her bike. Then she won't need to take yours.

JERRY: That's a great idea! Thanks for the advice, Rita.

3 Answer the questions.

a. Is Rita Jerry's sister or his friend?

b. Why was Jerry angry?

c. Why did Jerry's sister take his bike?

d. Why was Jerry's sister angry?

e. What two pieces of advice did Rita give Jerry?

Building Vocabulary

4 **Vocabulary Check** Match the verbs with the correct meaning.

_____ **1.** to let
_____ **2.** to trust
_____ **3.** to ask for permission
_____ **4.** to complain
_____ **5.** to worry
_____ **6.** to drive someone crazy
_____ **7.** to give advice
_____ **8.** to get mad

a. to say something is not right
b. to be afraid or nervous
c. to ask for someone's OK
d. to permit, to allow
e. to believe in
f. to become angry
g. to bother or annoy
h. to suggest what to do about a problem

Synonyms

Some words in English have similar meanings. We call them synonyms.

| big—large | seat—chair | smart—intelligent |

5 Read about Sandy. Find a synonym for each word in parentheses. Use words from the box.

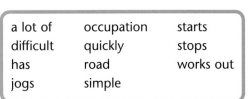

a lot of	occupation	starts
difficult	quickly	stops
has	road	works out
jogs	simple	

Sandy's day **(1.)** ___*starts*___ at
        (begins)
seven in the morning. She drives to

work on a busy **(2.)** _____. She
        (street)
likes her **(3.)** _____ and she has
       (job)
(4.) _____ friends at work.
   (many)
Usually, the work is **(5.)** _____
           (easy)
for her, but sometimes it is

(6.) _____. Every afternoon, she **(7.)** _____ working
   (hard)   (finishes)
at five o'clock. She drives home **(8.)** _____ and changes her
                                 (fast)
clothes. She **(9.)** _____ and then she **(10.)** _____ for
        (exercises)   (runs)
half an hour. After that, she **(11.)** _____ dinner with her family and
                       (eats)
watches TV.

Talk About It

 6 Work with a partner. Think of a problem you had in the past. Were you worried about something? Was someone driving you crazy? Tell your partner about your problem. Ask your partner questions.

Example:

A: I had a problem when I was about fourteen years old.

B: What kind?

A: I had problems with my big brother. I was always taking his things, and he got mad at me. I guess I was really driving him crazy.

B: What did you do about it?

GRAMMAR

Reflexive Pronouns

We use reflexive pronouns when the subject and the object are the same.

Singular	Plural
I cut **myself**.	Did **you** see **yourselves** on TV?
Did **you** hurt **yourself**?	**We** saw **ourselves** in the mirror.
She talks to **herself**.	**They** heard **themselves** on tape.
He laughed at **himself**.	
It turns **itself** on.	

Reflexive pronouns can also mean "alone" or "without help." In this case, they sometimes come after the word *by*.

I went to the movies **by myself**.	She fixed the bike **herself**.

1 Answer the questions.

a. Irene went to Chicago alone. Who went to Chicago? _____*Irene*_____ How did she go? ___*by herself*___

b. No one was home, so Betty made a cup of tea. Who made the tea? _____ Who did she make it for? _____

c. Randy and Mike made this doghouse without help. Who made the doghouse? _____ How did they make it? _____

d. Tom looked in the mirror. Who looked in the mirror? _____ Who did he look at? _____

e. Nitza is learning how to sew. She made that skirt. Who made the skirt? _____ How did she make it? _____

2 Complete the sentences with the correct reflexive pronouns.

   a. Alfredo isn't studying tai chi with a teacher. He's teaching _____.

   b. I have to remember a lot of things, so I write _____ notes.

   c. My stove turns _____ off when the food is hot.

   d. Kyle and Mariko didn't hurt _____ in the accident.

   e. We're going to paint the bedroom by _____.

   f. That's a beautiful photograph. Did you take it _____?

3 Complete the sentences with the correct reflexive pronoun. Use *by* if possible.

   a. Maribel is a good cook. She made dinner ___*by herself*___.

   b. Jiraporn loves to study. She is learning English _____.

   c. If I buy chocolate, I'll eat all of it. I don't trust _____.

   d. Did you write this _____? It's very good!

   e. I prefer to go shopping _____.

   f. You work out every day and you eat well. You take good care of _____.

   g. Mia is proud of _____ because she got an A in biology.

4 Complete the sentences with one of the verbs in the box and a reflexive pronoun.

cut	take care of
buy	turn off
teach	

   a. Bob is trying to _____ how to speak French before he goes to France.

   b. Newborn kittens cannot _____ if the mother cat leaves them.

   c. Be careful with that knife. You might _____.

   d. Whenever she gets paid, Maja likes to _____ a new pair of shoes.

   e. Don't worry about the lights. They _____ at midnight.

5 **Express Yourself** Work in small groups. Talk about how you spend your free time. Then complete the chart on page 122 with favorite activities. Do you prefer to do them by yourselves or with other people? Make a check mark (✓) for each person for each activity.

Example:

A: What do you like to do in your free time?

B: I like to take photographs. I usually take them by myself.

A: So do I.

C: I don't. I like to go with a friend when I take photographs.

Favorite activities	Do by ourselves	Do with others
1. *Taking photographs*	✓✓	✓
2.		
3.		
4.		
5.		
6.		

6 What was the most popular activity to do by yourselves? What was the most popular activity to do with other people? Tell the class.

LISTENING and SPEAKING

Listen: "Hello, You're on *Health Line.*"

1 On some radio programs, an expert gives advice to listeners with problems. Do you ever listen to that kind of radio program? What is your opinion of this kind of program?

STRATEGY **2** **Before You Listen** You will hear part of a radio "call-in" show. The guest is a skin doctor, and he's giving advice to two teenagers. What problems do teenagers often have with their skin?

3 Listen to the radio program. Who do Claire and Jerome have problems with? Circle the answers.

   a. Claire has problems with   her mother   her friends   boys.

   b. Jerome has problems with   his parents   his friends   girls.

4 Look at the list below. All of these things can affect your skin. Listen to the program again. Which eight things does Dr. Nemo talk about? Check (✓) the boxes.

☐ drinking water   ☐ getting enough sleep
☐ eating chocolate and french fries ☐ smoking
☐ eating fruits and vegetables   ☐ swimming
☐ eating whole grains   ☐ taking medicine
☐ exercising   ☐ washing your face
☐ lying in the sun   ☐ wearing makeup

Pronunciation

Unstressed *he, him, her,* and *his*

These words drop the **"h"** sound when they are inside a phrase. They link to the word that comes before them.

Is he here?

You should ask him.

What's her name?

He washed his face.

 5 Listen and repeat these sentences.

- **a.** Jerry's sister took his bicycle.
- **b.** Jerry didn't hear her.
- **c.** She got mad at him.
- **d.** She wanted her brother's help.
- **e.** Was he sorry?

 6 Mark these sentences in the same way. Practice them aloud. Then listen and check your pronunciation.

- **a.** Rita gave him good advice.
- **b.** Did he listen to her? (2 links)
- **c.** They're going to fix her bike.
- **d.** He's going to ask her to help him. (2 links)
- **e.** He needs help with his French.

Speak Out

 Giving Advice You can use these expressions to give advice.

Why don't you talk to her?

How about telling them the truth?

If you trust him, **maybe** he'll change.

7 Work with a partner. You are teenagers and you have problems with your parents. Or you are parents (of different families) who have problems with your teenagers. First, think about your "problem." How can you explain it to someone? Then tell each other your problems and give advice.

Example:

A: My son is driving me crazy. He talks on the phone all the time. Nobody can call us because he's always using it. And he doesn't have time for his homework.

B: Why don't you talk to him about it?

A: I did, but it didn't help. And I know he needs to talk to his friends.

B: How about telling him he can use the phone for only one hour a day? Maybe between 7:00 p.m. and 8:00 p.m.

A: That's good advice. Maybe that will work.

READING and WRITING

Read About It

 1 **Before You Read** Do you ever read the advice column in a magazine or newspaper? Why or why not? Do you usually agree with the answers?

ASK KIT AND KAT

Kit   **Kat**

Dear Kit and Kat:

The most popular girl in school, Andrea, invited me to a party, but she didn't invite my best friend Barbara. I didn't even tell Barbara about the party because I don't want to hurt her feelings.

Today Barbara invited me to go to Disney World with her family on the same weekend as the party. I didn't really say yes or no, and I think that hurt her. I would love to go to Disney World, but I don't want to miss the party, and I don't want to lose Barbara as a friend.

I have to give her an answer soon. What can I say?

Confused

Dear Confused:

Do you really like Andrea? Or do you just want to be with the popular kids? And what about Barbara? Do you really care about her? Or do you just want to go to Disney World?

I don't know the answers to these questions, but you know them. You're confused because you want to have everything, and that's not possible. You need to figure out what's really important to you and make a choice.

Kit

Dear Confused:

Talk to Andrea. Maybe she forgot to invite Barbara. Explain that it's difficult for you if she doesn't ask Barbara. Maybe Barbara will go to the party, or maybe she'll go to Disney World, but she'll feel better if Andrea invites her.

Kat

Dear Kit and Kat:

Our teenage son is driving us crazy! He gets home at about six o'clock and starts talking to his friends on the phone. If we let him, he talks for three or four hours. We can't use the phone, and he isn't doing his homework.

We asked him to be more considerate, but he didn't listen. We made a rule that he can only talk on the phone for one hour every day, but now we have an argument every time the phone rings. He's angry, we're angry—everyone is unhappy. What can we do with this kid?

Mad Dad

Dear Mad Dad:

Get your son his own telephone number—and make him pay for it himself!

Kit

Dear Mad Dad:

It sounds like you have more problems than just the telephone. Your son knows he's driving you crazy, and it looks like he wants to.

I think you need to talk with your son about his place in the family and the rules you make for him. You need to agree about what's fair. If your son feels that the rules are fair, he'll probably follow them.

Kat

 STRATEGY **Getting the General Idea** If you understand the general idea of a reading, it's easier to figure out the specific ideas and to guess new words.

2 Circle the correct answers.

1. The letter from "Confused" is about a problem with
   a. friends　　　**b.** her family　　　**c.** her school work

2. Kit and Kat give "Confused"
   a. the same advice　　**b.** different advice

3. The letter from "Mad Dad" is about a problem with
   a. his telephone　　**b.** his son　　　**c.** his wife

4. Kit and Kat give "Mad Dad"
   a. the same advice　　**b.** different advice

Vocabulary Check Match these expressions with their meanings. Write the letters on the lines.

1. _____ to agree   **a.** to choose
2. _____ to be considerate   **b.** to be careful
3. _____ to be fair   **c.** to make someone sad or upset
4. _____ to feel   **d.** to believe, to think
5. _____ to figure something out   **e.** to say what someone has to do
6. _____ to hurt someone's feelings   **f.** to think the same
7. _____ to make a choice   **g.** to find the answer
8. _____ to make a rule   **h.** to be OK

Think About It

 Work in small groups. Discuss these questions.

a. Do you agree with Kit's and Kat's advice to "Confused"? Which advice do you think is better? What advice would you give "Confused"?

b. Do you agree with Kit's and Kat's advice to "Mad Dad"? Which advice do you think is better? What advice would you give "Mad Dad"?

Write About It

When you ask for advice, you need to do three things: 1) explain the situation; 2) explain your problem; and 3) ask for advice.

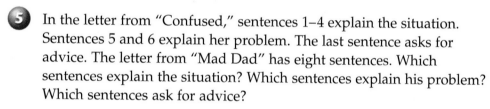 In the letter from "Confused," sentences 1–4 explain the situation. Sentences 5 and 6 explain her problem. The last sentence asks for advice. The letter from "Mad Dad" has eight sentences. Which sentences explain the situation? Which sentences explain his problem? Which sentences ask for advice?

STRATEGY **6** **Before You Write** Think of a new problem or use one of the problems you discussed in Talk About It on page 120 or in Speak Out on page 123. Make notes about the situation and the problem.

7 **Write** Write a letter to Kit and Kat asking for advice. Use the same letter form as in the letters from "Confused" and "Mad Dad." Don't use your own name. Be careful with verb tenses. You will probably need both present and past forms.

 8 **Check Your Writing** Use the editing checklist below. Then work with a partner and check your partner's letter. Discuss any questions with your partner. Revise your letter if necessary.

- Did you describe the situation completely?
- Did you state your problem clearly?
- Did you use verb tenses correctly?

1 Complete the conversations. Use object pronouns, possessive pronouns, or reflexive pronouns.

Don: Lalo, that isn't your notebook.

Lalo: No, it isn't **(1.)** _____. I don't know who **(2.)** _____ belongs to.

Don: Maybe it belongs to that girl. She was just sitting here.

Lalo: Yeah, maybe it's **(3.)** _____.

Don: Then why don't you give it to **(4.)** _____?

Lalo: I'm too shy. You do it!

Don: Me? That's not my job, it's **(5.)** _____. You found the notebook.

Lalo: I can't just walk up to her by **(6.)** _____. Come with **(7.)** _____.

Don: No way! You give it to her **(8.)** _____.

2 Choose the correct clause to end each sentence. Write the letter of the ending on the line.

1. Linda doesn't lie, _____
2. If Linda studies hard, _____
3. Linda is very popular _____
4. When I saw Linda yesterday, _____
5. While her friends were talking, _____
6. If Linda is nice to other people, _____
7. Linda takes care of herself, _____
8. Linda was studying by herself _____

a. she was shopping with a friend.
b. when her friends surprised her.
c. they will be nice to her.
d. so she almost never gets sick.
e. she will get good grades.
f. so people trust her.
g. Linda was making a phone call.
h. because she is friendly to everyone.

3 Complete the conversation with the simple present or the present progressive of the verbs in parentheses.

Rae: What kind of vacation **(1. take)** _____ you _____ this year?

Tom: Well, I **(2. like)** _____ to ride horses so I usually **(3. go)** _____ out west somewhere. This year I **(4. go)** _____ to a ranch near the Grand Canyon in Arizona. I **(5. ride)** _____ to the bottom of the canyon and I **(6. camp)** _____ there for four days.

Rae: Wait a minute! What's the name of the ranch?

Tom: Canyon Ranch. Why?

Rae: I **(7. take)** _____ notes. It **(8. sound)** _____ great! I **(9. want)** _____ to go there some time.

4 Complete each sentence with the adverb form of the adjective in parentheses.

a. My father is a fast driver, but he drives very **(careful)** _____.

b. It's late, so I'll have to work **(fast)** _____.

c. The car hit the wall **(hard)** _____, but the driver was OK.

d. She doesn't play tennis **(good)** _____, but she's an excellent skater.

e. He spoke **(kind)** _____ to the frightened child.

f. We smiled **(happy)** _____ when the music started.

g. Look! I spelled my own name **(wrong)** _____!

h. He plays the violin **(beautiful)** _____, but he can't sing.

Vocabulary Review

Use the map. Complete the directions with the words in the box. You can use words more than once.

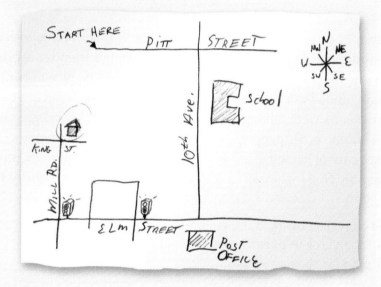

northeast	north	block	traffic light
northwest	south	right	post office
southeast	east	take	left
southwest	west	school	go
shopping center			

(1.) _____ Pitt Street to 10th Avenue. Go (2.) _____ on 10th to the (3.) _____. Turn (4.) _____ on Elm Street. Go to the second (5.) _____. That's Mill Road. Turn (6.) _____ and go one (7.) _____ to King Street. My house is on the (8.) _____ corner. It's gray.

Base Form	Simple Past	Base Form	Simple Past
be: am, is, are	was, were	hurt	hurt
become	became	keep	kept
begin	began	know	knew
break	broke	leave	left
bring	brought	lose	lost
build	built	make	made
buy	bought	mean	meant
catch	caught	meet	met
come	came	pay	paid
cut	cut	put	put
do	did	read	read
draw	drew	ride	rode
drink	drank	run	ran
drive	drove	say	said
eat	ate	see	saw
fall	fell	sell	sold
find	found	send	sent
fit	fit	sing	sang
fly	flew	sit	sat
forget	forgot	sleep	slept
get	got	speak	spoke
give	gave	stand	stood
go	went	swim	swam
grow up	grew up	take	took
have, has	had	think	thought
have to, has to	had to	understand	understood
hear	heard	win	won
hit	hit	write	wrote

THE INTERNATIONAL PHONETIC ALPHABET

IPA SYMBOLS

Consonants

/b/	baby, club	/s/	salt, medicine, bus
/d/	down, today, sad	/š/	sugar, special, fish
/f/	fun, prefer, laugh	/t/	tea, material, date
/g/	good, begin, dog	/θ/	thing, healthy, bath
/h/	home, behind	/ð/	this, mother, bathe
/k/	key, chocolate, black	/v/	very, travel, of
/l/	late, police, mail	/w/	way, anyone
/m/	may, woman, swim	/y/	yes, onion
/n/	no, opinion	/z/	zoo, cousin, always
/ŋ/	angry, long	/ž/	measure, garage
/p/	paper, map	/č/	check, picture, watch
/r/	rain, parent, door	/ǰ/	job, refrigerator, orange

Vowels

/ɑ/	on, hot, father	/o/	open, close, show
/æ/	and, cash	/u/	boot, do, through
/ɛ/	egg, says, leather	/ʌ/	of, young, sun
/ɪ/	in, big	/ʊ/	put, cook, would
/ɔ/	off, daughter, draw	/ə/	about, pencil, lemon
/e/	April, train, say	/ɚ/	mother, Saturday, doctor
/i/	even, speak, tree	/ɝ/	earth, burn, her

Diphthongs

/ɑɪ/	ice, style, lie	/ɔɪ/	oil, noise, boy
/ɑʊ/	out, down, how		

THE ENGLISH ALPHABET

Here is the pronunciation of the letters of the English alphabet, written in International Phonetic Alphabet symbols.

a	/e/	n	/ɛn/
b	/bi/	o	/o/
c	/si/	p	/pi/
d	/di/	q	/kyu/
e	/i/	r	/ɑr/
f	/ɛf/	s	/ɛs/
g	/ǰi/	t	/ti/
h	/eč/	u	/yu/
i	/ɑɪ/	v	/vi/
j	/ǰe/	w	/ˈdʌbəlˌyu/
k	/ke/	x	/ɛks/
l	/ɛl/	y	/wɑɪ/
m	/ɛm/	z	/zi/

UNIT 1

Nouns
athlete
baseball
basketball
bath
champion
day off
lifestyle
midnight
nothing
routine
schedule
shower

skateboard
tennis
tooth/teeth
vacation

Verbs
to brush
to comb
to exercise
to get dressed
to get ready
to get up
to practice

to put on
to skate
to try
to visit

Adjectives
busy
daily
excellent
typical

Adverbs
again
also

always
ever
never
often
seldom
sometimes
together
usually

Prepositions
after
before
during
next

UNIT 2

Nouns
football
movie
museum
party
soccer
spare time

Verbs
to enjoy
to hate
to hike
to prefer
to relax

to stay
to wash

Adjectives
ambitious
bored/boring
careful
competitive
confident
easygoing
enthusiastic
excited/exciting
friendly
funny

greedy
hardworking
jealous
lazy
mean
messy
outgoing
patient
proud
quiet
responsible
self-confident
shy
sloppy

smart
stubborn
talented

Adverbs
probably
really

Expressions
in common
let's
me neither
me, too
so do I
Why don't we?

UNIT 3

Nouns
agent
apartment
bathroom
bathtub
bed
bedroom
bookcase
closet
corner
couch

counter
cupboard
dining room
downstairs
dresser
floor
garage
hall
kitchen
lamp
living room

plan
refrigerator
rug
sink
stairs
stove
toilet
upstairs

Verbs
to keep
to share

Adverbs
both
enough
maybe
too

Prepositions
above
across from
behind
between
under

UNIT 4

Nouns
air
animal
architect
artist
biologist
boss
bridge
computer programmer
customer
engineer

flower
gardener
grass
photographer
travel agent
tree
trip
waiter/waitress

Verbs
to check
to cut

to design
to draw
to forget
to have to
to paint
to take care of
to use

Adjectives
artistic
creative

dangerous
dead
fresh
safe

Adverbs
almost
just
off
until

UNIT VOCABULARY

UNIT 5

Nouns
bank
check
drugstore
errand
favor
guest
invitation
library
medicine
napkin
neighbor
package
plate
post office
present
restaurant
request
skill
stamp
supermarket

Verbs
to bring
to cash
to deposit
to explain
to fail
to give
to help
to invite
to mail
to order
to pay
to pick up
to require
to sell
to send
to show

Adjectives
sure
urban

Adverbs
else

Expressions
Could you ... ?
Would you... ?
Would you mind...?
What's the matter?

UNIT 6

Nouns
audience
aunt
circus
college
company
cousin
event
language
life/lives
(mother)-in-law
neighborhood
nephew
niece
parent
performer
tradition
uncle

Verbs
to arrive
to begin
to die
to find
to finish
to get divorced
to get married
to grow up
to leave
to miss
to move
to perform
to retire
to return
to travel

Modal
could/couldn't

UNIT 7

Nouns
bag
bean
can
carrot
chicken
cup
dessert
dish
fork
glass
knife/knives
menu
oil
pepper
pound
protein
recipe
rice
salt
spoon
soup
vegetable
vegetarian
vitamin

Verbs
to add
to choose
to fry
to serve
to set (the table)
to smell
to sound
to stir
to taste

Adjectives
delicious
fried
grilled
special

Other
a bunch of
a few
a little
a lot of
a serving of
many
much

UNIT 8

Nouns
accident
ambulance
arm
cat
cell phone
dog
emergency
fault
finger
fire
fire/police
  department
fire engine
firefighter
foot
guest
head
knee
leg
noise
smoke
thumb
traffic
traffic light
truck
witness

Verbs
to break
to burn
to cross
to fall
to hit
to hurt
to shout
to speed
to trip on/over

Adjectives
broken
hurt
lucky
upset

Other
so
suddenly
toward
while

Expressions
in a hurry

UNIT 9

Nouns
backpack
bag
belt
boots
button
catalog
coat
collar
cotton
credit card
fall
glove
hat

jacket
leather
leggings
material
pocket
raincoat
sandals
shorts
silk
size
skirt
sleeve
sneakers
spring

style
suit
summer
sunglasses
swimsuit
tie
umbrella
underwear
winter
wool
zipper

Verbs
to fit
to go with

to look good
to try on

Adjectives
better
dark
expensive
inexpensive
light
medium
perfect
worse

Expressions
as ... as
in style

UNIT 10

Nouns
beach
block
boat
date
directions
east
forest
island
left
map

motorcycle
mountain
museum
nature
north
ocean
price
right
river
sailboat
south

surprise
tour
west
zoo

Verbs
to camp
to get (a place)
to go sightseeing
to hike
to rent
to sail
to turn

Adjectives
free (not busy)
included
wonderful

Prepositions
far from
near
through

Other
if

UNIT 11

Nouns
beginning
end
exhibit
key
middle
painting
part
photography
play
program
public
review
row

sculpture
seat
tickets
way
world

Verbs
to act
to belong
to change
to decide
to disturb
to express
to prefer
to start

Adjectives
abstract
empty
familiar
modern
popular
realistic

Adverbs
angrily
badly
clearly
fast
hard
loudly
slowly

softly
well

Possessive Pronouns
his
hers
mine
ours
theirs
yours

Other
Whose

Expressions
Excuse me
I'm sorry

UNIT 12

Nouns
advice
grade
makeup
mirror
permission
reason
road
skin
soap
synonym
teenager

Verbs
to affect
to ask for permission
to complain
to figure out
to give advice
to let
to lie
to make fun of
to nod
to protect
to shout

to stay out
to trust
to worry

Adjectives
considerate
fair
friendly
high
low
mad
popular

responsible
serious
simple

Adverbs
even
quickly
still

Expressions
to drive someone
  crazy
to get mad

INDEX

Numbers indicate units.

Adverbs. 11

Agreeing and disagreeing. 2, 8, 11

As + adjective + *as*. 9

Asking Questions About the Past 6

Better than/Worse than. 9

Clauses

   Before, after, when 4

   When, while. 8

   Because, so 8

   If. 10

Could/Couldn't. 6

Count/Non-count nouns 7

Direct and indirect objects 5

Do and *make*. 4

Dress and clothing. 9

Expressions with *time*. 8

Frequency adverbs. 1

Future tense with *will*. 3

Future with *be going to* 3

Gerunds 2

Getting the general idea 12

Getting the main idea 1, 8

Giving advice 12

Go + verb *–ing*. 10

Guess the meaning of new words. . . . 5

Have to/Has to. 4

How long/how long ago 6

I'm sorry/Excuse me 11

–ing and *–ed* adjectives 2

It + infinitive 2

Linking verbs. 7

Making suggestions. 2

Menus and food 7

Nouns used as adjectives 9

Occupations 4

Ordering from a catalog 9

Past progressive tense 8

Polite requests: *Could you/would you*. . 5

Possessive pronouns. 11

Prepositions of place: *in, on, at*. 3

Present progressive: future meaning   10

Reading a map 10

Reflexive pronouns. 12

Scanning. 3, 6, 9, 10

Sequence of adjectives. 9

Sequencing. 4

Simple present tense 1

Skimming 2

Spare-time activities. 2

Specific/non-specific quantities. 7

Synonyms 12

Take 1

Things in a house 3

Time expressions 1, 6

Too and *not ... enough* 3

Understanding the main ideas 1, 8

Understanding reference words 11

Vacations. 10

Whose. 11